ABIGAIL ADAMS
AND HER TIMES

Books By LAURA E. RICHARDS

ABIGAIL ADAMS

From an original painting by Gilbert Stuart

ABIGAIL ADAMS AND HER TIMES

BY
LAURA E. RICHARDS

AUTHOR OF "ELIZABETH FRY, THE ANGEL OF THE PRISONS,"
"FLORENCE NIGHTINGALE, THE ANGEL OF THE
CRIMEA," ETC.

ILLUSTRATED

D. APPLETON AND COMPANY
NEW YORK   LONDON
1928

CONTENTS

LIST OF ILLUSTRATIONS

For much of the local and contemporary color in this little book, the author is indebted to the admirable works of the late Mrs. Alice Morse Earle.

ABIGAIL ADAMS AND HER TIMES

CHAPTER I

BEGINS AT THE BEGINNING

SEVENTEEN HUNDRED AND FORTY-FOUR! George the Second on the throne of England, "snuffy old drone from the German hive"; Charles Edward Stuart ("bonnie Prince Charlie") making ready for his great *coup* which, the next year, was to cast down said George from the throne and set Charles Edward thereupon as "rightful, lawful prince—for wha'll be king but Charlie?", and which ended in Culloden and the final downfall and dispersion of the Scottish Stuarts.

In France, Louis XV., Lord of Misrule, shepherding his people toward the Abyss with what skill was in him; at war with England, at war with Hungary; Frederick of Prussia alone standing by him. In Europe, generally, a seething condition which is not our immediate concern. In America, seething also: discontent, indignation, rising higher and higher under British imposition (not British either, being the work of Britain's German ruler, not of her people!), yet quelled for the moment by war with France.

I am not writing a history; far from it. I am merely throwing on the screen, in the fashion of to-day, a few scenes to make a background for my little pen-picture-play. What is really our immediate concern is that on November eleventh of this same year, 1744, was born to the wife of the Reverend William Smith of Weymouth, Massachusetts, a daughter, baptized Abigail.

Parson Smith was a notable figure of the times; not a great man, but one of character, intelligence and cultivation. He married a daughter of Colonel John Quincy, so my heroine was a cousin—I cannot tell in what precise degree—to Dorothy Q. of poetic-pictorial fame; cousin, too, (her grandmother having been a Norton) to half Boston, the cultivated and scholarly half.

Parson Smith kept a diary, as dry a document as I have often read. He had no time to spare, and his brief entries are abbreviated down to the finest possible point. For example, we read that

"By my Gd I am as'd and Ev. am as'd at my S

and do now ys D Sol prom By Thy God never to T. to s. ag."

This is puzzling at first sight; but the practiced reader will, after some study, make out that the good Parson, writing for himself alone, was really saying,

"By my God I am assured and Even am assured at my Strength, and do now this Day Solemnly promise By Thy God never to Tempt to sin again."

Even this is somewhat cryptic, but we are glad of the assurance, the more that we find the poor gentleman still troubled in spirit a week later.

"Lord g't me S to res the e. so prej'd to me. Lord I am ashamed of it and resolve to s. e. T. by thy S."

Which being interpreted is: "Lord, grant me Strength to resist the evil so prejudicial to me. Lord, I am ashamed of it and resolve to shun evil Temptation by thy Strength."

What the temptation was, we may not know. Possibly he was inclined to extravagance in certain matters of personal dignity and adornment: we read of his paying fifteen pounds "for my wig"; and again, "At Boston. Paid Mr. Oliver for a cut whigg £10.00." But this is nothing. Parson Smith came of "kent folk," and may have had private means beside the salary of eight hundred dollars. Do we not read that Samuel Adams' barber's bill "for three months, shaving and dressing," was £175, paid by the Colony of Massachusetts?

Necessary expenses were also heavy. "Dec. 4th, 1749. Paid Brother Smith for a Barrel of Flower £15.11.3." But on the other hand, he sold his horse to Mr. Jackson for £200.

1751 was an eventful year. On April 23d we read,

"Weymouth Meeting House took fire about half an hour after 10 o'clock at night and burnt to the ground in abt 2 hours."

This is all Parson Smith has to say about it, but the Boston *Post-Boy* of April 29th tells us that:

"Last Tuesday Night the old Meeting-house in Weymouth was burnt to the Ground : and three Barrels of Gunpowder, the Town-Stock, being in the Loft, blew up with a great noise. 'Tis uncertain by what Means the Fire happen'd."

Paul Torrey, the town poet, says of it:

> Our powder stock, kept under lock,
>   With flints and bullets were
> By dismal blast soon swiftly cast
>   Into the open air.

The poem hints at incendiaries.

I'm satisfied they do reside
  Somewhere within the town:
Therefore, no doubt, you'll find them out,
  By searching up and down.

On trial them we will condemn,
  The sentence we will give:
Them execute without dispute,
  Not being fit to live.

This was a heavy blow to minister and congregation, in fact to the whole community; for the meeting-house was the centre and core of the village life.

Meeting-house: (Cotton Mather found "no just ground in Scripture to apply such a trope as 'church' to a home for public assembly.") Sabbath, or more often Lord's Day: these are the Puritan names, which happily we have not yet wholly lost. The early meeting-houses were very small; that of Haverhill was only twenty-six feet long and twenty wide. They were oftenest set on a hilltop, partly as a landmark, partly as a lookout in case of prowling Indians. The building or "raising" of a meeting-house was a great event in the community. Every citizen was obliged by law to share in the work or the expense. Every man must give a certain amount of "nayles." Contributions were levied for lumber, for labor of horses and men, and for "Rhum and Cacks" to regale the workers. "When the Medford people built their second meeting-house, they provided for the workmen and bystanders, five barrels of rum, one barrel of good brown sugar, a box of fine lemons, and two loaves of sugar. As a natural consequence, two-thirds of the frame fell, and many were injured. In Northampton, in 1738, ten gallons of rum were bought for £8 'to raise the meeting-house'—and the village doctor got '£3 for setting his bone Jonathan Strong, and £3 10s. for setting Ebenezer Burt's thy' which had somehow through the rum or the raising, both gotten broken." [1] Finally it was realized that rum and "raising" did not go well together, and the workmen had to wait till night for their liquor.

Once up, the meeting-house became the centre of village life. On the green outside stood the stocks, the whipping-post, the pillory, the cage. We are told that the first man to occupy the Boston stocks was the carpenter who made them, his charge for the lumber used being considered over high. The pillory was much frequented by Quakers and other non-orthodox persons. Here, too, were horse-blocks, and rows of stepping-stones for muddy days. The Concord horse-block was a fine one; it was

[1] "The Sabbath in Puritan New England." Alice Morse Earle.

erected by the women of the town, each housewife
giving a pound of butter toward the expense. On
the walls and door of the meeting-house were nailed
grinning heads of wolf and bear, killed partly for
safety, possibly more for the reward: fifteen shillings for a live wolf, ten for a dead one. We are not
told what was done with the live wolves. A man in
Newbury killed seven wolves in one year; but that is
nothing. We learn from the history of Roxbury
that in 1725, in one week in September, twenty bears
were killed within two miles of Boston! Wolves
were far more dreaded than bears, and save in this
one remarkable instance, far more abundant. In
1723, Ipswich was so beset by wolves that children
could not go to meeting or to school without a
grown attendant.

In the early days, the meeting-house was un-
painted; paint would have been thought a sinful
extravagance. The eighteenth century, however,
brought laxer ideas; brought also cheaper paint, and
the result was a sudden access of gayety. Pomfret,
Connecticut, painted its meeting-house bright yel-
low. Instantly Windham, near by, voted that its
meeting-house be "colored something like the Pomfret meeting-house." Killingly, in turn, gave orders
that "the cullering of the body of our meeting-

house should be like the Pomfret meeting-house, and the Roff shal be cullered Read." But Brooklyn carried off the palm, with a combination of orange, chocolate and white, which must have been startling even in 1762, and which would surely have sent Cotton Mather into convulsions, had he been alive to see.

Wolves' heads outside the meeting-house; inside, the village powder magazine! It was the safest place, because there was never any fire in the meeting-house. Sometimes in the steeple, sometimes under the roof-beams, there the "powder-closite" was. If a thunder-storm came on during service, the congregation ran out, and waited under the trees till it was over.

Few meeting-houses boasted a bell. The shrill toot of a horn, the clear blast of a conch-shell, or the roll of a drum, gave the signal for prayer, and brought the villagers hurrying from their doors and across the green to the meeting-house. In East Hadley, the man who "blew the cunk" received three dollars a year for his services. The drummer was better paid, receiving fourteen shillings of the town's money.

This digression on meeting-houses (drawn from Mrs. Alice Morse Earle's delightful "Sabbath in

Puritan New England") may be pardoned if it gives some idea of the disaster so briefly recorded by Parson Smith. Neither parson nor parishioners were one whit discouraged, however. On May 16th, it is true, they kept a "Fast, to bewail the burning of our Meeting House": but on August 7th we read: "Began to raise Weymouth Meeting House, 3 days and half about it." And on September 1st: "Met in our New Meeting House. I p(reache)d."

What heroic labor, what depth and height of earnest purpose, what self-denial and sacrifice, these eight brief words represent, we may well imagine, but Parson Smith gives us no help. The thing was done: there was no more to say.

About this time, we begin to find ominous entries in the diary, following one another in quick and grievous succession. On the same page that records (August 15th) "P'd £15 for my wig," we read, "Mr. Benjamin Bicknells Child Died of the throat Distemper." Two days later: "Mr. Pettee's Daughter Died of the Throat D. aged 5. Paid £4 for a hat for my Son."

Every day through the rest of the year they were dying, the little children, of what we may suppose was diphtheria, or some kindred affection. It was a dreadful time. On November 21st we read:

"Fast Day at Mr. Bayleys Parish on account of the throat Distemper prevailing there. Mr. Colton p'd from 2 Jer. 30 'In vain have I smitten yr c(hil-dre)n ye rec'd no Correction.' "

There had been a similar epidemic in 1735-6. In twelve months, nine hundred and eighty-four died of the distemper, by far the greater part under ten years of age—"the woful effects of Original Sin," remarks a pious writer of the time.

All this time little Abigail Smith has been waiting patiently in her cradle; now her turn has come. Re-markable woman as she was, perhaps the most strik-ing fact in her life was that she *lived*. Why or how any Puritan baby survived its tribulations, one hardly knows; that is, any baby born in winter, and late November is winter in New England. Within a few days of its birth, the baby was taken to the meeting-house to be baptized; the meeting-house, unwarmed, as we have seen, from year's end to year's end, the wolf Cold waiting to receive the poor lamb, with jaws opened wider than those that grin-ned on the outer walls of the building. This expedi-tion often completed the baby's earthly career. "Of Judge Sewall's fourteen children but three survived him, a majority dying in infancy; and of fifteen children of his friend Cotton Mather, but two sur-

vived their father.[2] We are not actually told that
the christening expedition killed them, but we may
infer it in many cases.

The baby slept in a hooded cradle; before going
to his christening, he must be carried upstairs, with
silver and gold in his hand, and "scarlet laid on his
head to keep him from harm." If he had fits or
rickets, he was largely dosed with snail-water. To
make the "admirable and most famous Snail-water"
you must "take a peck of garden Shel Snails, wash
them well in Small Beer, and put them in an oven
till they have done making a Noise, then take them
out and wipe them well from the green froth that is
upon them, and bruise them shels and all in a Stone
Mortar, then take a Quart of Earthworms, scower
them with salt, slit them, and—"[3] but perhaps you
do not wish to make Snail-water, even the most admirable and famous; and after all, we have no reason to think that Abigail Smith had rickets, though
she was a delicate child. She was not thought
strong enough to go to school; possibly in any case
it might not have been thought necessary for her.
The education of woman was little thought of in
those days; indeed, she herself says in one of her

[2] "Customs and Fashions in Old New England." Alice Morse
Earle.

[3] *Ibid.*

letters that it was fashionable to ridicule female learning. In another letter, written the year before her death, she says:

"My early education did not partake of the abundant opportunities which the present days offer, and which even our common country schools now afford. *I never was sent to any school.* I was always sick. Female education, in the best families, went no further than writing and arithmetic; in some few and rare instances, music and dancing."

How, then, did Abigail get her education? Easily enough; school was not necessary for her. She loved books, and there were plenty of them, not only in Parson Smith's study, but in the home of her grandfather, Colonel John Quincy, then living at Mount Wollaston, not far from Weymouth. A great part of her childhood was spent with her grandparents, and to her grandmother Quincy, in particular, she always felt that she owed a great deal.

"I have not forgotten," she writes to her own daughter in 1795, "the excellent lessons which I received from my grandmother, at a very early period of life. I frequently think they made a more durable impression upon my mind than those which I received from my own parents. Whether it was owing to the happy method of mixing instruction and amusement together, or from an inflexible adherence to certain principles, the utility of which I could not but see and approve when a child, I know not; but maturer years have rendered them oracles of wisdom to me. I love and revere her memory; her lively, cheerful disposition animated all around her, whilst she edified all by her unaffected piety. This tribute is due to the memory of those virtues the sweet remembrance of which will flourish, though she has long slept with her ancestors."

We can fancy the child sitting by the delightful grandmother, imbibing instruction and amusement, working the while at her sampler, or setting delicate stitches in a shirt for father or grandfather. Girls do not make the family shirts nowadays; but I know one dear lady who at seven years old was set down at her grandmother's side to cut and make a shirt for her grandfather, taking every stitch herself. We can see Abigail, too, browsing among Colonel Quincy's bookshelves; reading Shakespeare and Dryden and Pope and Prior; the *Spectator,* too, and all the history she could lay her hands on, and perhaps the novels of Mr. Richardson, Mr. Fielding, Mr. Smollett, three young men who were making a great stir in those days. She wrote letters, too, in the fashion of the time; endless letters to girl friends in Weymouth or Boston, "hifalutin" in language, but full of good sense and good feeling. We elders are always sighing, "Give us, ah! give us but yesterday!" and I cannot help deploring the decay of letter-writing. Says Charles Francis Adams, in the admirable Memoir with which he prefaces his collection of the letters of John and Abigail Adams:

"Perhaps there is no species of exercise, in early life, more productive of results useful to the mind, than that of writing letters. Over and above the mechanical facility of constructing sentences, which no teaching will afford so well, the interest with which the object is commonly pursued gives an extraordinary impulse to the intellect. This is promoted in a degree proportionate to the scarcity of temporary and local subjects for discussion. Where there is little gossip, the want of it must be supplied from books. The love of literature springs up where the weeds of scandal take no root. The young ladies of Massachusetts, in the last century, were certainly readers, even though only self-taught; and their taste was not for the feeble and nerveless sentiment, or the frantic passion, which comes from the novels and romances in the circulating library of our day, but was derived from the deepest wells of English literature. The poets and moralists of the mother country furnished to these inquiring minds their ample stores, and they were used to an extent which it is at least doubtful if the more pretending and elaborate instruction of the present generation would equal."

However this may be, (and I believe every word of it myself!) we must all be thankful that Abby Smith formed the letter-writing habit early in life; if she had not, we might have lacked one of the most vivid pictures of life in Revolutionary times. Her girlhood letters (those at least to her girl friends) were signed "Diana," and were addressed to Myra, Aspasia, Calliope, Aurelia. Later, in writing to her faithful friend, lover and husband, "Portia" was the name she chose, a name that suited her well. Here is a letter, written in her girlhood, to her friend, Mrs. Lincoln:

"Weymouth, 5 *October,* 1761.

"MY DEAR FRIEND,

"Does not my friend think me a stupid girl, when she has kindly offered to correspond with me, that I should be so senseless as not to accept the offer? Senseless and stupid I would confess myself, and

that to the greatest degree, if I did not foresee the
many advantages I shall receive from correspond-
ing with a lady of your known prudence and understanding.

"I gratefully accept your offer; although I may
be charged with vanity in pretending to entertain
you with my scrawls; yet I know your generosity is
such, that, like a kind parent, you will bury in ob-
livion all my imperfections. I do not aim at entertaining. I write merely for the instruction and edi-
fication which I shall receive, provided you honor
me with your correspondence. . . .

"You bid me tell *one* of my sparks (I think that
was the word) to bring me to see you. Why! I believe you think they are as plenty as herrings, when,
alas! there is as great a scarcity of them as there is
of justice, honesty, prudence and many other virtues. I've no pretensions to one. Wealth, wealth
is the only thing that is looked after now. 'Tis said
Plato thought, if Virtue would appear to the world,
all mankind would be enamoured with her, but now
interest governs the world, and men neglect the
golden mean.

"But, to be sober, I should really rejoice to come
and see you, but if I wait till I get a (what did you
call 'em?) I fear you'll be blind with age.

"I can say, in the length of this epistle, I've made the golden rule mine. Pray, my friend, do not let it be long before you write to your ever affectionate

"A. S."

One feels sure that Abigail was a good child, as well as a bright one. She was not an infant prodigy, one is glad to think; parents and grandparents were too sensible to play tricks with her mind or her soul. One sighs to read of the "pious and ingenious Jane Turell," a Puritan child who could relate many stories out of the Scriptures before she was two years old. "Before she was four years old, she could say the greater part of the Assembly's Catechism, many of the Psalms, read distinctly, and make pertinent remarks on many things she read. She asked many astonishing questions about divine mysteries." It is comforting to know that Jane liked green apples; her father, at the end of a pious letter adjures her "as she loves him not to eat them," but it shows that after all she was a human child.

We do not know much about the diet of Puritan children. Parson Smith was a good farmer, killed his own pork and beef, planted apple trees, made cider, etc. We may suppose that Abigail had plenty of good fish and flesh, with a "sallet" now and then, and corn, squash, and pumpkins at her desire. "Pompions," the latter were often called, while "squash" were variously known as squantersquash, askutasquash, isquoukersquash, all Indian variants of the one name which we clip into a monosyllable. Wheat did not grow well in the Colonies; oaten and rye meal was chiefly used in combination with the universal corn. They had hasty pudding, boiled in a bag, or fried: "sukquttahhash," and jonne-cake, or journey cake, which we have changed by the insertion of an *h* till it appears as if "Johnny" had either invented or owned it. Parched corn (our pop-corn), a favorite food of the Indians, was also highly appreciated by the Colonists. They were amazed at first sight of it: Governor Winthrop explains carefully how, on being parched, the corn turns entirely inside out, and is white and floury within. Sometimes they made it into "No-cake," which is, we are told, "Indian corn, parched in the hot ashes, the ashes being sifted from it; it is afterwards beaten to powder and put into a long leatherne bag, trussed like a knapsacke, out of which they take thrice three spoonfuls a day." This was considered wonderfully sustaining food; it was mixed, before eating, with snow in winter, with water in summer.

The pumpkins were made into "pyes," cakes, bread, sauce.

We have pumpkins at morning and pumpkins at noon,
If it were not for pumpkins we should be undone.

Potatoes were brought over from England as early as 1636, but were not grown till some time later. People were still afraid of them: some thought that "if a man eat them every day he could not live beyond seven years." Some again fancied the balls were the edible portion, and "did not much desire them." Nor were the recipes for cooking them specially inviting. "The Accomplisht Cook" much in use about the year 1700 says that potatoes must be "boiled and blanched; seasoned with nutmeg and cinnamon and pepper; mixed with eringo roots, dates, lemon, and whole mace; covered with butter, sugar, and grape verjuice, made with pastry; then iced with rosewater and sugar, and yclept a 'Secret Pye.'" [4]

Let us hope that Mrs. Smith, a Quincy born, knew better than to torture and overwhelm a worthy vegetable! We know little of this good lady, but

[4] "Customs and Fashions in Old New England." Alice Morse Earle.

we may suppose that she was a notable housewife, since her daughter in later life showed such skill in all household arts. We shall see by and by how Abigail baked and brewed, spun and wove, clothed and fed and cared for her family, often with little or no assistance. We may fancy her now, trotting about after Mother Smith at Weymouth or Grand-mother Quincy at Wollaston, her bright eyes noting everything, her quick fingers mastering all the arts of preserving, candying, distilling. There was a passion for such work among the New England women in those days.

"They made preserves and conserves, marmalets and quiddonies, hypocras and household wines, us-quebarbs and cordials. They candied fruits and made syrups. They preserved everything that would bear preserving. I have seen old-time receipts for preserving quinces, 'respasse,' pippins, 'apri-cocks,' plums, 'damsins,' peaches, oranges, lemons, artichokes; green walnuts, elecampane roots, eringo roots, grapes, barberries, cherries; receipts for syrup of clove gillyflower, wormwood, mint, ani-seed, clove, elder, lemons, marigold, citron, hyssop, liquorice; receipts for conserves of roses, violets, bo-rage flowers, rosemary, betony, sage, mint, lavender, marjoram, and 'piony'; rules for candying fruit, berries, and flowers, for poppy water, cordial, cherry water, lemon water, thyme water, Angelica water, Aqua Mirabilis, Aqua Celestis, clary water, mint water." [5]

Good living was cheap in Abigail's childhood. An English traveler, visiting Boston in 1740, writes thus: "Their poultry of all sorts are as fine as can be desired, and they have plenty of fine fish of various kinds, all of which are very cheap. Take the butchers' meat all together, in every season of the year, I believe it is about twopence per pound sterling; the best beef and mutton, lamb and veal are often sold for sixpence per pound of New England money, which is some small matter more than one penny sterling.

"Poultry in their season are exceeding cheap. As good a turkey may be bought for about two shillings sterling as we can buy in London for six or seven, and as fine a goose for tenpence as would cost three shillings and sixpence or four shillings in London. The cheapest of all the several kinds of poultry are a sort of wild pigeon, which are in season the latter end of June, and so continue until September. They are large, and finer than

[5] "Customs and Fashions in Old New England." Alice Morse Earle.

those we have in London, and are sold here for
eighteenpence a dozen, and sometimes for half of
that.

"Fish, too, is exceedingly cheap. They sell a fine
fresh cod that will weigh a dozen pounds or more,
just taken out of the sea, for about twopence sterling. They have smelts, too, which they sell as cheap
as sprats are in London. Salmon, too, they have in
great plenty, and these they sell for about a shilling
apiece, which will weigh fourteen or fifteen pounds."

Shad, strange to say, was profoundly despised.
In Puritan times they were fed to the hogs; in 1733
they sold two for a penny, and it was not at all "the
thing" to eat them—or at least to be seen eating
them! A story is told of a family in Hadley, Massachusetts, who were about to dine on a shad; and
who, hearing a knock at the door, delayed opening it
till shad and platter had been hustled out of sight.

"They have venison very plenty. They will sell
as fine a haunch for half a crown as would cost full
thirty shillings in England. Bread is much cheaper
than we have in England, but is not near so good.
Butter is very fine, and cheaper than ever I bought
any in London; the best is sold all summer for
threepence a pound. But as for cheese, it is neither
cheap nor good."

And milk was one penny a quart!

But we shall see great changes before we finish our story. These were the years of plenty, of the fat kine and the full ears of corn. Eat your fill, Abigail! drink your milk while it is a penny a quart; the lean years are coming, when you will pinch and scrape and use all your wit and ability to feed and clothe your family, and will look back with a sigh on these full years of your childhood.

CHAPTER II

GIRLHOOD AND MARRIAGE

WE are told that Abigail Smith in her childhood and girlhood was "surrounded by people of learning and political sagacity." Who were some of these people? At home in Weymouth, there was her father, of course, "remarkably lively and animated in all his public performances," as we learn from his tombstone. Doubtless his company was stimulating to the bright little girl; perhaps he took her with him now and then on his trips to Boston or Hingham, when he went to preach or to buy "Flower"; and ministers and other godly folk often came to the parsonage. But probably at her grandparents' home she saw even more people of learning and political sagacity. The Quincy clan itself made a goodly fellowship of cultivated men and women. The Hancocks lived near by. John Hancock was a boy of seven when Abigail was born. In the year 1755, when she was eleven, he was a lad of eighteen; had graduated the year before from Harvard

College and had already begun a brilliant mercan-
tile career. John was handsome and always fond
of good clothes and gay colors. We have no description of his youthful costumes, but we know
that one day in later life he wore "a red velvet cap
within which was one of fine linen, the last turned up
two or three inches over the lower edge of the velvet. He also wore a blue damask gown lined with
velvet, a white stock, a white satin embroidered
waistcoat, black satin small-clothes, white silk
stockings and red morocco slippers."

Roxbury was not far off, and here lived the War-
rens, warm friends of the Quincys. Joseph Warren
was three years younger than Abigail; they may
have played together in the Quincy gardens. We
may fancy them, the little maid in bib and apron,
mitts and kerchief; the little lad in flapped coat,
knee-breeches, and waist-coat reaching to his knees;
both have buckled shoes. Abby's hair is rolled
smoothly back over a cushion, Pompadour-fashion,
and tied behind with a ribbon; Joseph's worn in
much the same way, but without the cushion.

There was another young man named John, who
may have made calls either of ceremony or of
friendship at the Quincy mansion. John Adams
was a year behind John Hancock in college, having

graduated in this very year 1755, which I have chosen for a survey of my heroine's surroundings. He came of good New England stock, his father being a substantial farmer, and for many years a selectman of the town of Braintree. The Adamses were never rich, yet we are told that there had been a silver spoon in the family for four generations.

"In the year 1791, Miss Hannah Adams, the historian, in writing to John Adams, made reference to the 'humble obscurity' of their common origin. Her correspondent, in reply, while acknowledging the kinship, went on energetically to remark that, could he 'ever suppose that family pride were any way excusable, [he] should think a descent from a line of virtuous, independent New England farmers for a hundred and sixty years was a better foundation for it than a descent through royal or noble scoundrels ever since the flood.' " [1]

When young John was sixteen, his father offered him the choice of following the family pursuit of farming, and inheriting his share of the family estate, worth some thirteen hundred pounds, or of having a "learned education" for all his inheritance. There was no question of John Adams' choice; he

---

[1] "Three Episodes of Massachusetts History." C. F. Adams.

went to Harvard, as we have seen, and was one of the four best scholars in college at the time.

Shortly after receiving his degree, he became the teacher of the grammar school in the town of Worcester. This must have been a doleful change from his college life, with its gay and stimulating companionship, but he entered on the new work manfully, if not enthusiastically, and prospered in it.

Why do my thoughts so cluster round this year 1755? Why not take 1754, when Abigail was ten years old, or 1764, when she was twenty? Well, I shall have plenty to say about 1764, for that was the year—but never mind! The truth is, 1755 was a remarkable year, "a year never to be forgotten in America," [2] a year made memorable by the cruel expulsion of the French from Nova Scotia, by the destruction of General Braddock's army, by the unfortunate attempt of Sir William Johnson against Crown Point. These were incidents in the so-called French and Indian War, a war in some respects more dreadful than any other up to that of the present day; a war specially momentous for all Americans, since it was to pay the debts then contracted that Great Britain levied on the American Colonies (which had voluntarily spent vast sums

[2] "History of Massachusetts." Minot.

and suffered untold hardships in this war), the taxes which brought about the American Revolution.

So much from the historical point of view; but for myself, I must confess that two events, one actual and terrible, the other conjectural and delightful, fixed 1755 at an early age in my mind.

> That was the year when Lisbon town
> Saw the earth open and gulp her down.

I must have been a very small child when I proudly owned the Little Green Geography Book. There has been no other geography book like it; it was small, and square, and apple-green; it had many and wonderful pictures. Among these pictures, three impressed me most deeply: one of the Maelstrom, where a large vessel was going down over the edge of a terrifying circle like a round Niagara Falls; another of Peruvian Indians pulling up plants by the roots, and collecting quicksilver by the quart, it would appear. The third, and by far the most thrilling and terrifying, was of the Lisbon Earthquake. The ground was opening in every direction in long horrid chasms, and into these chasms were falling churches, houses, men, in dreadful confusion. This picture and that of the Maelstrom had a strange fascination for me; I was forever poring

over them, when I should have been learning about
the exports of Russia, of which to this day I can
give little account.

And then—but every one of my readers knows
that

> 'Twas on the terrible Earthquake Day
> That the Deacon finished the One Hoss Shay.

So it really is not surprising that 1755 is an *annus
mirabilis* to me.

It is interesting to find that the earthquake came
over seas to this country, and created considerable
disturbance, though no serious damage was done.
November the first was Lisbon's day of doom; it
was the eighteenth before the internal commotion
reached Massachusetts.

Parson Smith alludes to it with characteristic
brevity: "A great and terrible earthquake happened."

Six words! We can fancy Mrs. Smith rushing to
his study, crying out that the chimneys were falling,
that Neighbor Wibird's great elm was down; daughter Mary bringing the news that the "Chaney Tea-
pot had fallen from the dresser and was in a hundred pieces.

This, I say, we are at liberty to fancy, but Parson

Smith will not help us. His next entry is: "Married David Bicknell to Jerusha Vinsen. Lent the Dr. a pail of hair."

(No; I don't believe it was his wig; it was probably cattle hair, to use with mortar; but he does not say.)

John Adams is kinder to us. His diary begins thus:

"We had a very severe shock of an earthquake. It continued near four minutes. I then was at my father's in Braintree, and awoke out of my sleep in the midst of it. The house seemed to rock and reel and crack, as if it would fall in ruins about us. Chimneys were shattered by it within one mile of my father's house."

John Adams' diary is as different from that of his future father-in-law as cheese from chalk. No abbreviations here; no dry statistics of birth, death, marriage, as if they were of no human interest. He pours out his rolling periods with evident enjoyment. His son, who edits the diary, says:

"These are loose fragments of journal in the hand-writing of John Adams upon scraps of paper scarcely legible, from 18 November, 1755, to 20 November, 1761. They were effusions of mind, committed from time to time to paper, probably without the design of preserving them; self-examinations at once severe and stimulative; reflections upon others, sometimes, not less severe upon his friends; thoughts such as occur to all, some of which no other than an unsullied soul would commit to writing, mingled with conceptions at once comprehensive and profound."

The future President was already deeply interested in public affairs; his ardent patriotism was already forecasting the future of his beloved country. Shortly before the beginning of the Diary, he writes to his friend and kinsman, Nathan Webb:

"All that part of creation which lies within our observation, is liable to change. Even mighty states and kingdoms are not exempt. . . . Soon after the Reformation, a few people came over into this new world for conscience's sake. Perhaps this apparently trivial incident may transfer the great seat of empire into America. It looks likely to me; for if we can remove the turbulent Gallicks, our people, according to the exactest computation, will in another century become more numerous than England itself. Should this be the case, since we have, I may say, all the naval stores of the nation in our hands, it will be easy to obtain the mastery of the seas; and then the united force of all Europe will not be able

to subdue us. The only way to keep us from setting up for ourselves is to disunite us. *Divide et im-
pera.* Keep us distinct colonies, and then, some
great men in each colony desiring the monarchy of
the whole, they will destroy each others' influence
and keep the country in *equilibrio*.

"Be not surprised that I am turned politician.
This whole town is immersed in politics. The interests of nations, and all the *dira* of war, make the
subject of every conversation. I sit and hear, and
after having been led through a maze of sage ob-
servations, I sometimes retire, and by laying things
together, form some reflections pleasing to myself.
The produce of one of these reveries you have read
above. . . .

"Friendship, I take it, is one of the distinguishing
glories of man; and the creature that is insensible
of its charms, though he may wear the shape of
man, is unworthy of the character. In this, perhaps,
we bear a nearer resemblance to unembodied intelli-
gences than in anything else. From this I expect
to receive the chief happiness of my future life; and
am sorry that fortune has thrown me at such a distance from those of my friends who have the highest place in my affections. But thus it is, and I must
submit. But I hope ere long to return, and live in

that familiarity that has from earliest infancy sub-
sisted between yourself and affectionate friend,

                    "JOHN ADAMS."

We shall see about this. Friendship played an
important part in John Adams' life; but it was not
to form the chief happiness of his life.

He did not enjoy teaching; witness another letter to Nathan Webb.

"The situation of the town is quite pleasant, and
the inhabitants, as far as I have had opportunity
to know their character, are a sociable, generous,
and hospitable people; but the school is indeed a
school of affliction. A large number of little runt-
lings, just capable of lisping A B C, and troubling
the master. But Dr. Savil tells me, for my comfort,
'by cultivating and pruning these tender plants in
the garden of Worcester, I shall make some of them
plants of renown and cedars of Lebanon.' However
this be, I am certain that keeping this school any
length of time, would make a base weed and ignoble
shrub of me."

Yet at times he realized the value of his work.
We read in the diary of 1756:

"I sometimes in my sprightly moments consider
myself, in my great chair at school, as some dicta-

tor at the head of a commonwealth. In this little
state I can discover all the great geniuses, all the
surprising actions and revolutions of the great
world, in miniature. I have several renowned generals but three feet high, and several deep projecting
politicians in petticoats. I have others catching and
dissecting flies, accumulating remarkable pebbles,
cockle-shells, etc., with as ardent curiosity as any
virtuoso in the Royal Society. Some rattle and thunder out A B C, with as much fire and impetuosity
as Alexander fought, and very often sit down and
cry as heartily upon being outspelt, as Cæsar did,
when at Alexander's sepulchre he reflected that the
Macedonian hero had conquered the world before
his age. At one table sits Mr. Insipid, foppling and
fluttering, spinning his whirligig, or playing with
his fingers, as gaily and wittily as any Frenchified
cox-comb brandishes his cane or rattles his snuff-
box. At another, sits the polemical divine, plodding
and wrangling in his mind about 'Adam's fall, in
which we sinned all,' as his Primer has it. In short,
my little school, like the great world, is made up of
kings, politicians, divines, L.D.'s, fops, buffoons, fid-
dlers, sycophants, fools, coxcombs, chimney-sweep-
ers, and every other character drawn in history, or
seen in the world. Is it not, then, the highest pleas-

ure, my friend, to preside in this little world, to be-
stow the proper applause upon virtuous and generous actions, to blame and punish every vicious and
contracted trick, to wear out of the tender mind
everything that is mean and little, and fire the new-
born soul with a noble ardor, and emulation?"

Out of school hours, John Adams was studying
law with all possible diligence. By 1758 he was able
to give up teaching, and was admitted to practise at
the Massachusetts bar. His ability was recognized
at once. A few years later, Governor Barnard,
wishing to attach this promising young lawyer to
the royal party, offered him the office of advocate-
general in the Admiralty Court, which was considered a sure step to the highest honors of the bench.

This was the young man who, in 1764, came
knocking at the door of Parson Smith of Weymouth, asking the hand of his daughter Abigail in
marriage; to whom she writes on April 20th:

"I hope you smoke your letters well, before you
deliver them. Mamma is so fearful lest I should
catch the distemper, that she hardly ever thinks the
letters are sufficiently purified. Did you never rob
a bird's nest? Do you remember how the poor bird
would fly round and round, fearful to come nigh,
yet not know how to leave the place? Just so they

say I hover round Tom, whilst he is smoking my
letters.

"But heyday, Mr. What's your name, who taught
you to threaten so violently? 'A character besides
that of a critic, in which if I never did, I always
hereafter shall fear you.' Thou canst not prove a
villain, impossible,—I, therefore, still insist upon it,
that I neither do nor can fear thee. For my part, I
know not that there is any pleasure in being feared;
but, if there is, I hope you will be so generous as to
fear your Diana, that she may at least be made
sensible of the pleasure. Mr. Ayers will bring you
this letter and the *bag*. Do not repine,—it is filled
with balm.

"Here is love, respects, good wishes, regards—a
whole wagon load of them, sent you from all the
good folks in the neighborhood.

"Tomorrow makes the fourteenth day. How
many more are to come? I dare not trust myself
with the thought. Adieu. Let me hear from you
by Mr. Ayers, and excuse this very bad writing; if
you had mended my pen it would have been better.
Once more, Adieu. Gold and silver have I none,
but such as I have give I unto thee,—which is the
affectionate regard of your

"A. S."

ABIGAIL ADAMS
From an early portrait

We know little of the preliminary steps in the courtship. The young lawyer, riding his circuit, naturally passed through Weymouth, perhaps rode directly by the house of Parson Smith. The parson doubtless knew the elder Adams, would naturally offer civility and hospitality to his son; a man of parts himself, he would quickly perceive the intelligence and character of the young lawyer. But the Family at Large was mightily disturbed. Lawyers were looked askance at in those days; the law was a new profession, probably a dangerous, possibly an iniquitous one. Quincys, Nortons, Tynes, all shook their heads emphatically. The whole parish followed suit. What! Abigail, with her wit, beauty, gentle blood and breeding, marry "one of the dishonest tribe of lawyers," the son of a small country farmer? Perish the thought!

The elder sister Mary had been married the year before to Richard Cranch. This was thought a wholly suitable match. Parson Smith preached a wedding sermon, taking for his text, "And Mary hath chosen that good part, which shall not be taken away from her," and everybody was pleased. But no one, except the contracting parties and the Parson, seems to have approved of Abigail's marrying John Adams. This, however, troubled none of the three overmuch. It is true that John had to do his courting without assistance from his future "in-laws." He must tie his horse to a tree and find his Abigail as he could: no one even offered him a courting-stick, that "hollow stick about an inch in diameter and six or eight feet long, fitted with mouth and ear pieces" [3] through which some lovers, seated on either side of the great fireplace, had to carry on their courtship in the presence of the whole family.

Possibly John Adams might have declined this privilege even had it been offered. He has nothing to say about his courtship, but thus soberly and gravely he writes of his marriage.

"Here it may be proper to recollect something which makes an article of great importance in the life of every man. I was of an amorous disposition, and, very early, from ten or eleven years of age, was very fond of the society of females. I had my favorites among the young women, and spent many of my evenings in their company; and this disposition, although controlled for seven years after my entrance into college, returned and engaged me too much till I was married.

[3] "Customs and Fashions in Old New England." Alice Morse Earle.

"I shall draw no characters, nor give any enumeration of my youthful flames. It would be considered as no compliment to the dead or the living. This, I will say:—they were all modest and virtuous girls, and always maintained their character through life. No virgin or matron ever had cause to blush at the sight of me, or to regret her acquaintance with me. . . .

"I passed the summer of 1764 in attending courts and pursuing my studies, with some amusement on my little farm, to which I was frequently making additions, until the fall, when, on the 25th day of October, I was married to Miss Smith, second daughter of the Rev. William Smith, minister of Weymouth, granddaughter of the Honorable John Quincy, of Braintree, a connection which has been the source of all my felicity, although a sense of duty, which forced me away from her and my children for so many years, produced all the griefs of my heart, and all that I esteem real afflictions in life."

So they were married, and the parson conveyed a gentle reproof to his family and parishioners by preaching a sermon from Luke vii:33: "For John came neither eating bread nor drinking wine, and ye say, '*He hath a devil.*'"

CHAPTER III

THE BOSTON MASSACRE

IT was not a gay wedding, this of Abigail Smith and John Adams. They were married quietly by good Parson Smith, and then, hand in hand, walked across the fields to the little lean-to farmhouse where they were to find so much happiness and to live through such difficult times. It seems unlikely that Abigail enjoyed the pretty Colonial custom of "coming out Bride," of which we read in old diaries and letters. On the first Sunday after the wedding it was customary for the bride and groom, "whether old or young, gentle or simple," to go to church in the very best finery they could muster. If they were well-to-do, they kept this up for the four Sundays of the honeymoon, sometimes—oh, un-Puritan extravagance!—in a new gown and suit each time!

"They usually arrived a bit late, in order to have their full meed of attention; and proceeded slowly, arm in arm, down the broad aisle to seats of honor,

in the hushed attention of the entire congregation.
. . . At a certain point in the services, usually after
the singing of the second hymn, the happy couple, in
agonies of shyness and pride, rose to their feet, and
turned slowly twice or thrice around before the eyes
of the whole delighted assembly, thus displaying to
the full every detail of their attire." [1]

This would not have suited either Abigail or John
Adams. Their tastes were simple, their minds set
on far other things than clothes. Mrs. Adams was
always neat and trim in her dress, never extravagant
or ostentatious. Whether in the little Braintree
farmhouse, at the Court of St. James, or as Lady of
the White House, she was always the same—simple, modest, dignified: an example and an inspiration to all around her.

The first ten years of her married life were passed
happily and quietly, partly in Braintree, partly in
Boston, whither Mr. Adams' increasing law practice often called him. Four children were born to
her, a daughter named for herself, and three sons,
John Quincy, Charles and Thomas.

Mrs. Adams kept no diary; it is to her husband's
that we naturally turn for records of these ten

[1] "Two Centuries of Costume in America." Alice Morse
Earle.

years of happy family life. Alas! he has nothing to say about them. He was *living* his home life; it never occurred to him to write about it. His diary is concerned with public and professional affairs, and with them alone.

It was not till forced apart by the pressure of public duties and private service, that these two loving hearts needed any other expression than the spoken word of affection, cheer and sympathy. It is to the breaking up of their happy home life that we owe the Familiar Letters which are of such priceless value to all students of American history, to all lovers of high and noble thought.

But we have not come to the separation yet; we must consider these ten silent years, and fill in the picture as best we may.

Here is a sketch, boldly drawn by John Adams himself, writing in his old age to a friend, which brings the time before us as nothing else can. He is describing a scene in the Council Chamber in the old Town House, in February, 1761.

"In this chamber, round a great fire, were seated five judges, with Lieutenant Governor Hutchinson at their head as Chief Justice, all arrayed in their new, fresh, rich robes of scarlet English broadcloth; in their large cambric bands and immense judicial wigs. . . . In this chamber were seated at a long table all the barristers at law of Boston, and of the neighboring county of Middlesex in gowns, bands, and tie wigs. They were not seated on ivory chairs, but their dress was more solemn and pompous than that of the Roman Senate, when the Gauls broke in upon them. . . .

"Samuel Quincy and John Adams had been admitted barristers at that term. John was the youngest; he should be painted looking like a short, thick archbishop of Canterbury, seated at the table with a pen in his hand, lost in admiration.

"But Otis was a flame of fire, with . . . a torrent of impetuous eloquence, he hurried away everything before him. . . . Then and there the child Independence was born."

The year 1763 is usually regarded as the beginning of the American Revolution, since it was in that year that George III and his ministers determined to raise a revenue from the colonies. These matters belong rather to history than to biography, but we must briefly note the most striking events of this important time. In 1761 were issued the Writs of Assistance, which empowered Government officials to enter and search the houses of citizens for possible contraband goods. In 1765 came the Stamp

Act, imposing war-taxes on the Colonies, and struck cold on the hearts of the colonists. Franklin, seldom stirred out of his philosophic calm, cried aloud on hearing of it, "The sun of liberty is set!" For John Adams, it was the call to action, and from it dates his entrance into the field of politics. He was a selectman of Braintree at this time: "he prepared at home a draft of instructions, and carried them with him to the meeting. They were accepted by the town without a dissenting voice, and being published in Draper's paper, from a copy furnished to the printer at his request, were adopted by forty other towns of the province, as instructions to their respective representatives. Passages from them were also adopted in the instructions from the town of Boston to their representatives, which were drawn up by Samuel Adams."

Immediately after the Boston town meeting, John Adams was asked to appear as counsel for the town before the governor and council, "in support of the memorial of the town, praying that the courts of law in the province" (closed by order of the governor, because the stamps had not been delivered) might be opened.

Singularly enough, on the same evening, possibly at the same hour, when the people of Boston were thus showing their trust and confidence in him, Mr. Adams was recording in his diary the doubts and fears which beset him at the prospect opened before him by the Stamp Act and its consequences.

"The bar seem to me to behave like a flock of shot pigeons; they seem to be stopped; the net seems to be thrown over them, and they have scarcely courage left to flounce and to flutter. So sudden an interruption in my career is very unfortunate for me. I was but just getting into my gears, just getting under sail, and an embargo is laid upon the ship. Thirty years of my life are passed in preparation for business; I have had poverty to struggle with, envy and jealousy and malice of enemies to encounter, no friends, or but few, to assist me; so that I have groped in dark obscurity, till of late, and had but just become known and gained a small degree of reputation, when this execrable project was set on foot for my ruin as well as that of America in general, and of Great Britain."

On receiving the invitation from Boston next day, he marveled.

"When I recollect my own reflections and speculations yesterday, a part of which were committed to writing last night, and may be seen under December 18th, and compare them with the proceedings of

Boston yesterday, of which the foregoing letter informed me, I cannot but wonder, and call to mind Lord Bacon's observation about secret invisible laws of nature, and communications and influences between places that are not discovered by sense.

"But I am now under all obligations of interest and ambition, as well as honor, gratitude and duty, to exert the utmost of my abilities in this important cause. How shall it be conducted?"

As we all know, the Stamp Act was repealed in March, 1776, and we find no more doubts or fears in John Adams' diary. Henceforth he belonged to his country. So did the diary! From now on it is chiefly a record of public affairs. This was natural, but one does wish he had said a little more about his home and family. Only now and then do we find an entry of this kind:

"A duller day than last Monday, when the Province was in a rapture for the repeal of the Stamp Act, I do not remember to have passed. My wife, who had long depended on going to Boston, and my little babe, were both very ill, of an whooping cough. Myself under obligation to attend the superior court at Plymouth the next day, and therefore unable to go to Boston, and the town of Braintree insensible to the common joy!"

Or we read: "Set off with my wife for Salem; stopped half an hour at Boston, crossed the ferry, and at three o'clock arrived at Hill's, the tavern in Malden, the sign of the Rising Eagle, at the brook near Mr. Emerson's meeting-house, five miles from Norwood's: where, namely, at Hill's, we dined. Here we fell in company with Kent and Sewall. We all oated at Martin's, where we found the new sheriff of Essex, Colonel Saltonstall. We all rode into town together. Arrived at my dear brother Cranch's about eight, and drank tea, and are all very happy. Sat and heard the ladies talk about ribbon, catgut, and Paris net, ridinghoods, cloth, silk and lace. Brother Cranch came home, and a very happy evening we had."

Mr. Cranch was the gentleman in marrying whom Mary Smith had "chosen the good part." The brothers-in-law were warm friends and there were many pleasant family meetings.

"April 8th. Mounted my horse, in a very rainy morning, for Barnstable, leaving my dear brother Cranch and his family at my house. Arrived at Dr. Tufts', where I found a fine wild goose on the spit, and cranberries stewing in the skillet for dinner. Tufts, as soon as he heard that Cranch was at Braintree, determined to go over and bring him and wife and child over, to dine upon wild goose, and cranberry sauce."

In the spring of 1768, Mr. Adams moved into Boston with his wife and children. It was the first of several moves, which he thus records in his diary four years later:

"In April, 1768, I removed to Boston, to the white house in Brattle Square. In the spring, 1769, I removed to Cole Lane, to Mr. Fayerweather's house. In 1770, I removed to another house in Brattle Square, where Dr. Cooper now lives; in 1771, I removed from Boston to Braintree, in the month of April, where I have lived to this time. I hope I shall not have occasion to remove so often for four years and a half to come."

In 1768, John Adams went on circuit as usual. Returning, he found the town full of troops. They had landed "about one o'clock at noon, October the first, under cover of the ship's cannon, without molestation; and, having effected it, marched into the Common with muskets charged, bayonets fixed, drums beating, fifes playing, etc., making, with the train of artillery, upward of seven hundred men." [2]

The diary continues: "Through the whole succeeding Fall and Winter, a regiment was exercised

[2] "Gordon's History."

by Major Small, in Brattle Square, directly in front of my house. The spirit-stirring drum and the ear-piercing fife aroused me and my family early enough every morning, and the indignation they excited, though somewhat soothed, was not allayed by the sweet songs, violins and flutes, of the serenading Sons of Liberty under my windows in the evening. In this way and a thousand others, I had sufficient intimations that the hopes and confidence of the people were placed in me as one of their friends; and I was determined that, so far as depended on me, they should not be disappointed; and that if I could render them no positive assistance at least I would never take any part against them.

"My daily reflections for two years, at the sight of these soldiers before my door, were serious enough. Their very appearance in Boston was a strong proof to me, that the determination in Great Britain to subjugate us was too deep and invet-erate ever to be altered by us; for every thing we could do was misrepresented, and nothing we could say was credited. On the other hand, I had read enough in history to be well aware of the errors to which the public opinions of the people were liable in times of great heat and danger, as well as of the ex-travagances of which the populace of cities were capable when artfully excited to passion, and even when justly provoked by oppression. . . .

"The danger I was in appeared in full view before me; and I very deliberately, and, indeed, very solemnly, determined at all events to adhere to my principles in favor of my native country, which, indeed, was all the country I knew, or which had been known by my father, grandfather, or great grandfather; but, on the other hand, I never would deceive the people, nor conceal from them any essential truth, nor, especially, make myself subservient to any of their crimes, follies, or eccentricities. These rules, to the utmost of my capacity and power, I have invariably and religiously observed to this day."

The drummings and fifings were to have more serious results than the disturbing of good citizens' slumbers. The presence of the troops in Boston proved a constant and growing irritation to the citizens, already exasperated by repeated aggressions. The soldiers saw no reason why they should be polite to the people, the people saw every reason why they should be rude to the soldiers. There were constant wrangles and jangles, growing more and more frequent, more and more violent, till at length, on the night of March 5th, 1770, the seething pot boiled over. John Adams writes:

"The evening of the fifth of March I spent at Mr. Henderson Inches' house, at the south end of Boston, in company with a club with whom I had been associated for several years. About nine o'clock we were alarmed with the ringing of bells, and, supposing it to be the signal of fire, we snatched our hats and cloaks, broke up the club, and went out to assist in quenching the fire, or aiding our friends who might be in danger. In the street we were informed that the British soldiers had fired on the inhabitants, killed some and wounded others, near the town-house. A crowd of people was flowing down the street to the scene of action. When we arrived, we saw nothing but some field-pieces placed before the south door of the town-house, and some engineers and grenadiers drawn up to protect them. . . . Having surveyed round the town house, and seeing all quiet, I walked down Boylston Alley into Brattle Square, where a company or two of regular soldiers were drawn up in front of Dr. Cooper's old church, with their muskets all shouldered, and their bayonets all fixed. I had no other way to proceed but along the whole front in a very narrow space which they had left for passengers. Pursuing my way, without taking the least notice of them, or they of me, any more than if they had been marble statues, I went directly home to Cole Lane."

What had happened was the Boston Massacre, which is vividly described by John Quincy Adams, at that time a child of two years.

It was nine o'clock of a moonlight night, he tells us, and there had been a light fall of snow on the icy streets. A single sentry was pacing slowly up and down before the door of the custom house in King Street. From his beat he could hear shouts and tumult in the neighboring streets; Boston did not go to bed at curfew these days. Parties of citizens had met parties of soldiers, and exchanged uncomplimentary remarks, with shouts and threats on either side. Probably the sentry thought little of this: it went on every night, more or less. Presently, however, round the corner came a barber's boy, and began to "slang" the sentry himself. This was another matter, and he responded in kind. The dispute ran high; other boys came running, and with them men, angry men who had had their fill of British insolence. The sentry, who for his part had had quite enough of "rebel impudence," called for support, and out came a corporal and six men (or twelve— the accounts vary) under the direction of Captain

Preston, and ranged themselves in a semi-circle in front of his post. Instantly, as if by magic, the soldiers were surrounded by "forty or fifty of the lower order of town's people, who had been roving the streets armed with billets of wood. . . . What begins with jeering and profanity not seldom ends in some shape or other of deepest tragedy. Forty or fifty of the coarsest people of a small trading town and eight hirelings of an ordinary British regiment can scarcely be imagined as types of any solid principle or exalted sentiment, and yet at the bottom lay the root of bitterness which soon afterwards yielded such abundant fruit. This was the first protest against the application of force to the settlement of a question of right."

We all know the outcome. Seven of the soldiers, "either under orders or without orders," fired: five men fell mortally wounded: six others were wounded less seriously. Each musket was loaded with two balls and every ball took effect. "So fatal a precision of aim, indicating not a little malignity, though it seems never to have attracted notice, is one of the most singular cirumstances attending the affray. No wonder, then, that peaceable citizens of a town, until now inexperienced in events of the kind, should, in their horror of the spectacle, have called the act a massacre, and have demanded, in tones the most absolute, the instantaneous removal of the cause. The armed hand, which had done this deed, was that of England. It was not that of a friend or guardian. The drops of blood then shed in Boston were like the dragon's teeth of ancient fable—the seeds, from which sprung up the multitudes who would recognize no arbitration but the deadly one of the battle-field."

There can have been little sleep that night for either Mr. or Mrs. Adams. The latter was in delicate health. The roll of the drums, the shouts of "Town-born, turn out, turn out!" the tramp of soldiers, as company after company was hurried to the scene of action, must have been terrifying enough. Still the tumult grew, till at length Lieutenant-Governor Hutchinson, with great difficulty making himself heard from the balcony of the town house (now known as the Old State House) pledged his word to the citizens that justice should be done, and prevailed upon the commander of the troops to withdraw them to their barracks.

This quieted the tumult, but still a crowd of anxious citizens—not the rioters, but the sober patriots who realized the gravity of the crisis—besieged the closed doors behind which Governor and Commander and justices of the peace were in council. All night they waited, watchful, silent: at three in the morning, it was announced that Captain Preston had surrendered himself and was committed to prison; then, and not till then, Boston went to bed.

The rest of the story must be told by John Adams himself.

"The next morning, I think it was, sitting in my office, near the steps of the town-house stairs, Mr. Forrest came in, who was then called the Irish Infant. I had some acquaintance with him. With tears streaming from his eyes, he said, 'I am come with a very solemn message from a very unfortunate man, Captain Preston, in prison. He wishes for counsel, and can get none. I have waited on Mr. Quincy, who says he will engage, if you will give him your assistance; without it, he positively will not. Even Mr. Auchmuty declines, unless you will engage.' I had no hesitation in answering that counsel ought to be the very last thing that an accused person should want in a free country; that the bar ought, in my opinion, to be independent and impartial, at all times and in every circumstance, and that persons whose lives were at stake ought to have the counsel they preferred. But he must be sensible this would be as important a cause as was ever tried in any court or country of the world; and that every lawyer must hold himself responsible not only to his country, but to the highest and most infallible of all tribunals, for the part he should act. He must, therefore, expect from me no art or address, no sophistry or prevarication, in such a cause, nor any thing more than fact, evidence, and law would justify. 'Captain Preston,' he said, 'requested and desired no more; and that he had such an opinion from all he had heard from all parties of me, that he could cheerfully trust his life with me upon those principles.' 'And,' said Forrest, 'as God Almighty is my judge, I believe him an innocent man.' I replied, 'That must be ascertained by his trial, and if he thinks he cannot have a fair trial of that issue without my assistance, without hesitation, he shall have it.'

"Upon this, Forrest offered me a single guinea as a retaining fee, and I readily accepted it. From first to last I never said a word about fees, in any of those cases, and I should have said nothing about them here, if calumnies and insinuations had not been propagated that I was tempted by great fees and enormous sums of money. Before or after the trial, Preston sent me ten guineas, and at the trial of the soldiers afterwards, eight guineas more, which were all the fees I ever received or were offered to me, and I should not have said anything on the subject to my clients if they had never offered me anything. This was all the pecuniary reward I ever had for fourteen or fifteen days' labor in the most exhausting and fatiguing causes I ever tried, for hazarding a popularity very general and very hardly earned, and for incurring a clamor, popular suspicions and prejudices, which are not yet worn out, and never will be forgotten as long as the history of this period is read.

"It was immediately bruited abroad that I had engaged for Preston and the soldiers, and occasioned a great clamor, which the friends of the government delighted to hear, and slily and secretly fomented with all their art."

Their arts were of little avail. While the trial (which lasted through a whole term) was still in progress, an election came on for a representative of Boston, in the town meeting, and the people, eager to show their confidence in John Adams, elected him by a large majority.

"I had never been at a Boston town meeting, and was not at this, until messengers were sent to me to inform me that I was chosen. I went down to Faneuil Hall, and in a few words expressive of my sense of the difficulty and danger of the times, of the importance of the trust, and of my own insufficiency to fulfill the expectations of the people, I accepted the choice. Many congratulations were offered, which I received civilly, but they gave no joy to me. I considered the step as a devotion of my family to ruin, and myself to death; for I could scarce perceive a possibility that I should ever go through the thorns and leap all the precipices before me and escape with my life.

"At this time I had more business at the bar than any man in the Province. My health was feeble. I was throwing away as bright prospects as any man ever had before him, and I had devoted myself to endless labor and anxiety, if not to infamy and to death, and that for nothing, except what indeed was and ought to be all in all, a sense of duty. In the evening, I expressed to Mrs. Adams all my apprehensions. That excellent lady, who has always encouraged me, burst into a flood of tears, but said she was very sensible of all the danger to her and to our children, as well as to me, but she thought I had done as I ought; she was very willing to share in all that was to come, and to place her trust in Providence."

These apprehensions were unfounded. Thanks

to Adams' eloquence, Preston was acquitted, and so great was the public confidence in his advocate that not a murmur of dissent was heard, nor was his popularity in any degree lessened.

John Adams seldom condescends to anecdote, but he does tell us of "a labored controversy, between the House and the Governor, concerning these words: 'In General Court assembled, and by the authority of the same.' I mention this merely on account of an anecdote, which the friends of government circulated with diligence, of Governor Shirley, who then lived in retirement at his seat in Roxbury. Having read this dispute, in the public prints, he asked, 'Who has revived those old words? They were expunged during my administration.' He was answered, 'The Boston seat.' 'And who are the Boston seat?' 'Mr. Cushing, Mr. Hancock, Mr. Samuel Adams, and Mr. John Adams.' 'Mr. Cushing I knew, and Mr. Hancock I knew,' replied the old Governor, 'but where the devil this brace of Adamses came from, I know not.' This was archly circulated by the ministerialists, to impress the people with the obscurity of the original of the *par nobile fratrum,* as the friends of the country used to call us, by way of retaliation."

CHAPTER IV

THE BOSTON TEA PARTY

EVEN though it has little to say about his domestic life, I linger over John Adams' diary. It is enthralling reading; most of it belongs rather to history than to a slight record like this, yet here and there we get pleasant glimpses of the man himself.

Here he is on circuit, riding through Maine, which was then Massachusetts.

"Began my journey to Falmouth in Casco Bay. . . . Dined at Goodhue's, in Salem, where I fell in company with a stranger, his name I knew not. . . . One year more, he said, would make Americans as quiet as lambs; they could not do without Great Britain, they could not conquer their luxury, etc. Oated my horse, and drank balm tea at Treadwell's in Ipswich, where I found Brother Porter, and chatted with him half an hour, then rode to Rowley and lodged at Captain Jewett's. Jewett 'had rather the House should sit all the year round, than give up

been out of credit with me. Could I borrow the powers and faculties of my much valued friend, I should then hope to use it with advantage to myself and delight to others. Incorrect and unpolished as it is, I will not suffer a mistaken pride so far to lead me astray as to omit the present opportunity of improvement. And should I prove a tractable scholar, you will not find me tardy.

"You, madam, are so sincere a lover of your country, and so hearty a mourner in all her misfortunes, that it will greatly aggravate your anxiety to hear how much she is now oppressed and insulted. To you, who have so thoroughly looked through the deeds of men, and developed the dark designs of a rapacious soul, no action however base or sordid, no measure, however cruel and villanous, will be matter of any surprise.

"The tea, that baneful weed, is arrived. Great and, I hope, effectual opposition has been made to the landing of it. To the public papers I must refer you for particulars. You will there find that the proceedings of our citizens have been united, spirited and firm. The flame is kindled, and like lightning it catches from soul to soul. Great will be the devastation, if not timely quenched or allayed by some more lenient measures. Although the mind is shocked at the thought of shedding human blood, more especially the blood of our countrymen, and a civil war is of all wars the most dreadful, such is the present spirit that prevails, that if once they are made desperate, many, very many of our heroes will spend their lives in the cause, with the speech of Cato in their mouths.

"Such is the present situation of affairs, that I tremble when I think what may be the direful consequences, and in this town must the scene of action lie. My heart beats at every whistle I hear, and I dare not express half my fears. Eternal reproach and ignominy be the portion of all those who have been instrumental in bringing these fears upon me. There has prevailed a report that tomorrow there will be an attempt to land this weed of slavery. I will then write further. Till then, my worthy friend, adieu."

During ten days more, Abigail Adams' heart was to "beat at every whistle she heard." The patriots meant to make no mistakes in this important matter. They steadfastly refused to receive the tea; they used their utmost efforts to induce Governor Hutchinson to allow its return. It was not till all had been done that man could do, that the final step was taken and the tea disposed of. Trevelyan, in his history of the American Revolution, says: "Boston, under circumstances which have been too frequently described to admit of their ever again being related in detail, gratified the curiosity of an energetic patriot who expressed a wish to see whether tea could be made with salt water." It is the only passage in that admirable work with which I have a quarrel. Boston born and bred, I cannot be expected to pass over the Tea Party with a brief word. I must recall, if only for the sake of that beating heart of Abigail Adams', that scene on the night of December 16th: the painted figures stealing from street and alley and crooked lane to the rendezvous at the Old South Church; the war-whoop ringing out, the rush down Franklin Street to Griffin's Wharf; the shouts and laughter, under which lay such deadly earnestness; the scuffle on the decks, the splash! splash! as chest after chest of best Bohea and Hyson (to the value of eighteen thousand pounds) dropped into the icy water, and went "sailing so merrily out to sea." How should I not call up the scene at least thus briefly, when my own great-grandfather was one of the Mohawks? And how do we know that little Abigail and John Quincy Adams were not singing, in the days of turbulent excitement that followed the Tea Party, songs

something like the following, though this is of a
somewhat later date:

> There was an old lady lived over the sea,
>   And she was an Island Queen.
> Her daughter lived off in a new countrie
>   With an ocean of water between.
> The old lady's pockets were full of gold,
>   But never contented was she,
> So she called on her daughter to pay her a tax
>   Of three-pence a pound on her tea,
>   Of three-pence a pound on her tea.
>
> "Now, mother, dear mother," the daughter replied,
>   "I shan't do the thing you ax.
> I'm willing to pay a fair price for the tea,
>   But never the three-penny tax."
> "You shall," quoth the mother, and reddened with rage,
>   "For you're my own daughter, you see.
> And sure 'tis quite proper the daughter should pay
>   Her mother a tax on her tea,
>   Her mother a tax on her tea."
>
> And so the old lady her servant called up
>   And packed off a budget of tea,
> And, eager for three-pence a pound, she put in
>   Enough for a large familee.
> She ordered her servant to bring home the tax,
>   Declaring her child should obey,
> Or old as she was, and almost woman grown,
>   She'd half whip her life away,
>   She'd half whip her life away.
>
> The tea was conveyed to the daughter's door,
>   All down by the ocean side,

And the bouncing girl poured out every pound
  In the dark and boiling tide,
And then she called out to the Island Queen,
  "Oh! Mother! Dear Mother!" quoth she,
"Your tea you may have when 'tis steeped enough,
  But never a tax from me,
  No, never a tax from me!"[1]

The diary has little more to say than Trevelyan. We read "Twenty-eight chests of tea arrived yesterday, which are to make an infusion in water at seven o'clock this evening." And the next day: "Last night twenty-eight chests and a half of tea were drowned."

It is clear that Mr. Adams knew what was to be done; he never knew the names of the doers, steadfastly refusing to be told. "You may depend upon it," he says, writing to a friend in 1819, "that they were no ordinary Mohawks. The profound secrecy in which they have held their names, and the total abstinence from plunder, are proofs of the characters of the men. I believe they would have tarred and feathered anyone of their number who should have been detected in pocketing a pound of Hyson."

The following year, 1774, was a momentous one. The destruction of the tea had roused George III and his ministers to frenzy; they bent all their ener-

[1] Author unknown.

gies to punish the rebellious town of Boston. Edict followed edict. The Five Intolerable Acts, they were called. This is not the place to name them; be it merely said that one of them amounted practically to a repeal of the Charter of Massachusetts. Early in May General Gage arrived, with full powers as Civil Governor of the Colony, and as Commander-in-Chief for the whole continent, to see that the edicts were carried out. First came the Boston Port Bill, which closed the harbor of Massachusetts and transferred the business of the custom-house to Salem.

On May 26th, 1774, Governor Gage informed the General Court that its sessions would be held at Salem from June first till further orders. The court obeyed, met at Salem, under the leadership of Samuel Adams, and proceeded to make arrangements for a general congress at Philadelphia. Gage, hearing of this, sent a messenger post haste to Salem to dissolve the meeting. The messenger found the door locked, nor was it opened till the congress had been determined upon, and the Massachusetts committee appointed: James Bowdoin, Samuel Adams, John Adams, Thomas Cushing, Robert Treat Paine. This was on June 17th, 1774. On the same day, a great meeting was held at Faneuil Hall, with John Adams as moderator to protest against the iniquitous Port Bill.

Jonathan Sewall, John Adams' bosom friend, was a strong Royalist. On hearing of Adams' nomination to the projected Congress, he hastened to protest against his accepting it, with all the eloquence of which he was master. Every school child knows the answer by heart.

"I know," said John Adams, "that Great Britain has determined on her system, and that very fact determines me on mine. You know I have been constant and uniform in opposition to her measures; the die is now cast; I have passed the Rubicon; to swim or sink, live or die, survive or perish with my country, is my unalterable determination."

Meantime, on June 1st, the blockade of Boston Harbor was proclaimed, and the ruin and starvation of the city zealously undertaken. "I'll put Boston seventeen miles from the sea!" Lord North had vowed, and he was better than his word.

"The law was executed with a rigour that went beyond the intentions of its authors. Not a scow could be manned by oars to bring an ox, or a sheep, or a bundle of hay, from the islands. All water carriage from pier to pier, though but of lumber, or bricks, or kine, was forbidden. The boats that plied between Boston and Charlestown could not ferry a parcel of goods across Charles River. The fishermen of Marblehead, when they bestowed quintals of dried fish on the poor of Boston, were obliged to transport their offerings in wagons by a circuit of thirty miles." [2]

The British troops, which had been removed after the "Massacre," came back into the town, "sore and surly," [3] and encamped on Boston Common. The evil days had begun. Small wonder that under such conditions as these, John Adams' heart was heavy at leaving his home, even on so high an errand as that which called him to Philadelphia.

A month before this, he was writing to his wife the first of the famous Familiar Letters. It is dated Boston, 12 May, 1774.

"I am extremely afflicted with the relation your father gave me of the return of your disorder. My own infirmities, the account of the return of yours, and the public news coming all together have put my utmost philosophy to the trial.

"We live, my dear soul, in an age of trial. What will be the consequence, I know not. The town of

[2] "History of the United States of America." Bancroft.
[3] "The American Revolution." Trevelyan.

Boston, for aught I can see, must suffer martyrdom. It must expire. And our principal consolation is, that it dies in a noble cause—the cause of truth, of virtue, of liberty, and of humanity, and that it will probably have a glorious resurrection to greater wealth, splendor and power, than ever.

"Let me know what is best for us to do. It is expensive keeping a family here, and there is no prospect of any business in my way in this town this whole summer. I don't receive a shilling a week. We must contrive as many ways as we can to save expenses; for we may have calls to contribute very largely, in proportion to our circumstances, to prevent other very honest worthy people from suffering for want, besides our own loss in point of business and profit.

"Don't imagine from all this that I am in the dumps. Far otherwise. I can truly say that I have felt more spirits and activity since the arrival of this news than I had done before for years. I look upon this as the last effort of Lord North's despair, and he will as surely be defeated in it, as he was in the project of the tea.

"I am, with great anxiety for your health,

"Your   JOHN ADAMS."

Abigail was probably visiting in the country at this time; but shortly after, John moved his family once more to Braintree, "to prepare myself as well as I could for the storm that was coming on." He rode his circuit as usual, but for the last time. His letters are full of foreboding; full also of courage, and resolve to meet whatever fate held in store.

"Let us, therefore, my dear partner, from that affection which we feel for our lovely babes, apply ourselves, by every way we can, to the cultivation of our farm. Let frugality and industry be our virtues, if they are not of any others. And above all cares of this life, let our ardent anxiety be to mould the minds and manners of our children. Let us teach them not only to do virtuously, but to excel. To excel, they must be taught to be steady, active, and industrious."

He is not too anxious to give his usual keen attention to all he sees and hears. From York he writes:

"This town of York is a curiosity, in several views. The people here are great idolaters of the memory of their former minister, Mr. Moody. Dr. Sayward says, and the rest of them generally think, that Mr. Moody was one of the greatest men and best saints who have lived since the days of the

Apostles. He had an ascendency and authority over the people here, as absolute as that of any prince in Europe, not excepting his Holiness.

"This he acquired by a variety of means. In the first place, he settled in the place without any contract. His professed principle was that no man should be hired to preach the gospel, but that the minister should depend upon the charity, generosity, and benevolence of the people. This was very flattering to their pride, and left room for their ambition to display itself in an emulation among them which should be most bountiful and ministerial.

"In the next place, he acquired the character of firm trust in Providence. A number of gentlemen came in one day, when they had nothing in the house. His wife was very anxious, they say, and asked him what they should do. 'Oh, never fear; trust Providence, make a fire in the oven, and you will have something.' Very soon a variety of everything that was good was sent in, and by one o'clock they had a splendid dinner.

"He had also the reputation of enjoying intimate communication with the Deity, and of having a great interest in the Court of Heaven by his prayers.

"He always kept his musket in order, and was

fond of hunting. On a time, they say, he was out
of provisions. There came along two wild geese.
He takes gun and cries, 'If it please God I kill both,
I will send the fattest to the poorest person in this
parish.' He shot, and killed both; ordered them
plucked, and then sent the fattest to a poor widow,
leaving the other, which was a very poor one, at
home,—to the great mortification of his lady. But
his maxim was, Perform unto the Lord thy vow.

"But the best story I have heard yet was his doctrine in a sermon from this text, 'Lord, what shall
we do?' The doctrine was that when a person or
people are in a state of perplexity, and know not
what to do, they ought never to do they know not
what. This is applicable to the times."

On August 10th, Mr. Adams, with the other commissioners, took coach and started from Boston for
Philadelphia, escorted by enthusiastic crowds. From
this time, the Letters tell the story as nothing else
can. I therefore quote from them with only such
comment as may be necessary.

"The particulars of our journey I must reserve,
to be communicated after my return. It would
take a volume to describe the whole. It has been
upon the whole an agreeable jaunt. We have had
opportunities to see the world and to form acquaint-

ances with the most eminent and famous men in the several colonies we have passed through. We have been treated with unbounded civility, complaisance, and respect. We yesterday visited Nassau Hall College, and were politely treated by the scholars, tutors, professors, and president, whom we are this day to hear preach. Tomorrow we reach the theatre of action. God Almighty grant us wisdom and virtue sufficient for the high trust that is devolved upon us. The spirit of the people, whereever we have been, seems to be very favorable. They universally consider our cause as their own, and express the firmest resolution to abide by the determination of the Congress.

"I am anxious for our perplexed, distressed province; hope they will be directed into the right path. Let me entreat you, my dear, to make yourself as easy and quiet as possible. Resignation to the will of Heaven is our only resource in such dangerous times. Prudence and caution should be our guides. I have the strongest hopes that we shall yet see a clearer sky and better times.

"Remember my tender love to little Abby; tell her she must write me a letter and inclose it in the next you send. I am charmed with your amusement with our little Johnny. Tell him I am glad to

hear he is so good a boy as to read to his mamma
for her entertainment, and to keep himself out of
the company of rude children. Tell him I hope to
hear a good account of his accidence and nomencla-
ture when I return. . . .

"The education of our children is never out of
my mind. Train them to virtue. Habituate them
to industry, activity, and spirit. Make them consider every vice as shameful and unmanly. Fire
them with ambition to be useful. Make them disdain
to be destitute of any useful or ornamental knowledge or accomplishment. Fix their ambition upon
great and solid objects, and their contempt upon
little, frivolous, and useless ones. It is time, my
dear, for you to begin to teach them French. Every
decency, grace, and honesty should be inculcated
upon them. . . ."

ABIGAIL ADAMS TO JOHN ADAMS.

"I own I feel not a little agitated with the accounts I have this day received from town; great
commotions have arisen in consequence of a dis-
covery of a traitorous plot of Colonel Brattle's,—his
advice to Gage to break every commissioned officer
and to seize the province's and town's stock of gunpowder. . . .

"I should be glad to know how you found the people as you traveled from town to town. I hear you met with great hospitality and kindness in Connecticut. Pray let me know how your health is, and whether you have not had exceeding hot weather. The drought has been very severe. My poor cows will certainly prefer a petition to you, setting forth their grievances and informing you that they have been deprived of their ancient privileges, whereby they are become great sufferers, and desiring that they may be restored to them. More especially as their living, by reason of the drought, is all taken from them, and their property which they hold elsewhere is decaying, they humbly pray that you would consider them, lest hunger should break through stone walls.

"The tenderest regard evermore awaits you from your most affectionate

"ABIGAIL ADAMS."

"Braintree, 14 September, 1774.

"Five weeks have passed and not one line have I received. I would rather give a dollar for a letter by the post, though the consequence should be that I ate but one meal a day these three weeks to come. . . .

"We are all well here. I think I enjoy better health than I have done these two years. I have not been to town since I parted with you there. The Governor is making all kinds of warlike preparations, such as mounting cannon upon Beacon Hill, digging intrenchments upon the Neck, placing cannon there, encamping a regiment there, throwing up breast-works, etc. The people are much alarmed, and the selectmen have waited upon him in consequence of it. The County Congress have also sent a committee; all which proceedings you will have a more particular account of than I am able to give you, from the public papers. But as to the movements of this town, perhaps you may not hear them from any other person.

"In consequence of the powder being taken from Charlestown, a general alarm spread through many towns and was caught pretty soon here. The report took here on Friday, and on Sunday a soldier was seen lurking about the Common, supposed to be a spy, but most likely a deserter. However, intelligence of it was communicated to the other parishes, and about eight o'clock Sunday evening there passed by here about two hundred men, preceded by a horsecart, and marched down to the powder-house, from whence they took the powder, and carried it into the other parish and there secreted it. I opened the window upon their return. They passed without any noise, not a word among them till they came against this house, when some of them, perceiving me, asked me if I wanted any powder. I replied, no, since it was in so good hands. The reason they gave for taking it was that we had so many Tories here, they dared not trust us with it. . . . This town appears as high as you can well imagine, and, if necessary, would soon be in arms. Not a Tory but hides his head. The church parson thought they were coming after him, and ran up garret; they say another jumped out of his window and hid among the corn, whilst a third crept under his board fence and told his beads."

"The church parson" was probably the Rev. Anthony Wibird, of whom Mrs. Adams said, when on Fast Day, 1775, she drove to Dedham to church, that she did so because she "could not bear to hear our inanimate old bachelor." A few days after the burning of Falmouth she wrote, "I could not join today in the petition of our worthy pastor for a reconciliation between our no longer parent, but tyrant state and these colonies. Let us separate. They are not worthy to be our brethren. Let us renounce them, and instead of supplications, as formerly, for their prosperity and happiness, let us beseech the Almighty to blast their counsels and bring to naught all their devices."

"16 September.

"I have always thought it of very great importance that children should, in the early part of life, be unaccustomed to such examples as would tend to corrupt the purity of their words and actions, that they may chill with horror at the sound of an oath, and blush with indignation at an obscene expression. These first principles, which grow with their growth, and strengthen with their strength, neither time nor custom can totally eradicate."

JOHN ADAMS TO ABIGAIL ADAMS.

"Philadelphia, 20 September, 1774.

"I am anxious to know how you can live without Government. But the experiment must be tried. The evils will not be found so dreadful as you apprehend them. Frugality, my dear, frugality, economy, parsimony, must be our refuge. I hope the ladies are every day diminishing their ornaments, and the gentlemen, too. Let us eat potatoes and drink water; let us wear canvas, and undressed sheepskins, rather than submit to the unrighteous and ignominious domination that is prepared for us.

"Tell Brackett I shall make him leave off drinking rum. We can't let him fight yet. My love to my dear ones.

"Adieu."

A few days after this, Abigail writes, dating her letter "Boston Garrison, 24 September, 1774."

"I have just returned from a visit to my brother, with my father, who carried me there the day before yesterday, and called here in my return, to see this much injured town. I view it with much the same sensations that I should the body of a departed friend—having only put off its present glory for to rise finally to a more happy state. I will not despair, but will believe that, our cause being good, we shall finally prevail. The maxim 'In time of peace prepare for war' (if this may be called a time of peace) resounds throughout the country. Next Tuesday they are warned at Braintree, all above fifteen and under sixty, to attend with their arms; and to train once a fortnight from that time is a scheme which lies much at heart with many. . . .

"I left all our little ones well, and shall return to them tonight. I hope to hear from you by the return of the bearer of this, and by Revere. I long for the day of your return, yet look upon you as much safer where you are—but I know it will not do for you. Not one action has been brought to this court; no business of any sort in your way. All law ceases and the gospel will soon follow, for they are supporters of each other. Adieu."

In another letter she says: "All your family, too numerous to name, desire to be remembered. You will receive letters from two who are as earnest to write to papa as if the welfare of a kingdom depended upon it."

These two were little Abby and Johnny, who were missing their father sadly. One of John's letters reads thus:

"Sir—I have been trying ever since you went away to learn to write you a letter. I shall make poor work of it; but, sir, mamma says you will accept my endeavors, and that my duty to you may be expressed in poor writing as well as good. I hope I grow a better boy, and that you will have no occasion to be ashamed of me when you return. Mr. Thaxter says I learn my books well. He is a very good master. I read my books to mamma. We all long to see you. I am, sir, your dutiful son,

"JOHN QUINCY ADAMS."

It is pleasant to think of the little seven-year-old boy bending over his paper, laboriously composing this letter. He must have been a pretty boy, with his firm, clear-cut features. His dress was his father's in little, flapped waistcoat, knee breeches, buckled shoes, coat with cuffs and buttons and all the rest of it. I trust Mother Adams was too sensible to put him in a wig, but I do not know; most sons of well-to-do people wore wigs at that time. William Freeman was seven, just Johnny Adams' age, when his father paid nine pounds for a wig for him. Wigged or not, Johnny Adams knew how to write a letter. I wonder how many boys of seven could equal it today!

I cannot resist quoting another letter of Master Johnny's, written two years later.

"Braintree, June 2d, 1777.

"DEAR SIR:

"I love to receive letters very well; much better than I love to write them. I make but a poor figure at composition. My head is much too fickle. My thoughts are running after birds' eggs, play and trifles, till I get vexed with myself. Mamma has a troublesome task to keep me a-studying. I own I am ashamed of myself. I have but just entered the third volume of Rollin's Ancient History, but

designed to have got half through it by this time. I am determined this week to be more diligent. . . . I have set myself a stint this week, to read the third volume half out. If I can but keep my resolution, I may again at the end of the week give a better account of myself. I wish, sir, you would give me in writing, some instructions with regard to the use of my time, and advise me how to proportion my studies and play, and I will keep them by me, and endeavor to follow them. With the present determination of growing better, I am, dear sir, your son
"JOHN QUINCY ADAMS."

"P. S. If you will be so good as to favor me with a blank book, I will transcribe the most remarkable passages I meet with in my reading, which will serve to fix them upon my mind."

Johnny's taste in poetry was less mature. Writing in later years of these times, he says: "With these books (a copy of Shakespeare) in a closet of my mother's bedchamber, there was, (in 1778) also a small edition in two volumes of Milton's Paradise Lost, which I believe I attempted ten times to read, and never got through half a book. I might as well have attempted to read Homer before I had learned the Greek alphabet. I was mortified even to the shedding of solitary tears, that I could not even conceive what it was that my father and mother admired so much in that book, and yet I was ashamed to ask them an explanation. I smoked tobacco and read Milton at the same time, and from the same motive,—to find out what was the recondite charm in them which gave my father so much pleasure. After making myself four or five times sick with smoking, I mastered that accomplishment, and acquired a habit which, thirty years afterward, I had more difficulty in breaking off. But I did not master Milton. I was nearly thirty when I first read the Paradise Lost with delight and astonishment."

CHAPTER V

AFTER LEXINGTON

O N October 28th, Mr. Adams set out on his return homeward. The Diary reads:

"Took our departure, in a very great rain, from the happy, the peaceful, the elegant, the hospitable, and polite city of Philadelphia. It is not very likely that I shall ever see this part of the world again, but I shall ever retain a most grateful, pleasing sense of the many civilities I have received in it, and shall think myself happy to have an opportunity of returning them."

John Adams was to see a good deal more of Philadelphia; but he spent this winter of 1774-5 at home with Portia and the four children, happily, so far as home life went, but beset by anxieties and tasks. He was immediately elected into the Provincial Congress; besides this, he was writing weekly letters, signed "Novanglus," for the Boston *Gazette,* important letters answering those of "Massachusettensis" in Draper's paper, which "were conducted with a subtlety of art and address wonderfully calculated to keep up the spirits of their party, to depress ours, to spread intimidation, and to make proselytes among those whose principles and judgment give way to their fears; and these compose at least one-third of mankind." Mr. Adams notes soberly that "in New England, they [his own letters] had the effect of an antidote to the poison of Massachusettensis, and," he adds, "the battle of Lexington, on the 19th of April, changed the instruments of warfare from the pen to the sword."

Abigail, naturally, has nothing to say about Lexington and Concord; how should she? Her John was at home with her, and she kept no diary. But John *might* have given us a word about Paul Revere and the rising of the countryside, about the gathering of the minute-men on that green over which "the smoke of the battle still seems to hang": might have mentioned at least that toy pistol of Major Pitcairn's —a pretty thing, gold and mother-of-pearl, given him by admiring friends—which we are told fired the actual first shot of the Revolution, provoking that other which was "heard round the world": he might have told—as his son, long years after when he was President of the United States, loved to tell— how, the day after the battle, the minute-men came, and took Mrs. Adams' pewter spoons to melt them into bullets: but no!

"A few days after this event," he says, "I rode to Cambridge, where I saw General Ward, General Heath, General Joseph Warren, and the New England army. There was great confusion and much distress. Artillery, arms, clothing were wanting, and a sufficient supply of provisions not easily obtained. Neither the officers nor men, however, wanted spirits or resolution. I rode from thence to Lexington, and along the scene of action for many miles, and inquired of the inhabitants the circumstances. These were not calculated to diminish my ardor in the cause; they, on the contrary, convinced me that the die was cast, the Rubicon passed, and, as Lord Mansfield expressed it in Parliament, if we did not defend ourselves, they would kill us. On my return home, I was seized with a fever, attended with alarming symptoms; but the time was come to repair to Philadelphia to Congress, which was to meet on the fifth of May. I was determined to go as far as I could, and instead of venturing on horseback, as I had intended, I got into a sulky, attended by a servant on horseback, and proceeded on the journey."

This was an anxious journey for Mr. Adams,

knowing as he did, that he was leaving his beloved family exposed to many and grave dangers. Parliament had, in February, 1775, declared the Colony of Massachusetts to be in a state of rebellion, and things went from bad to worse in Boston. The following letter gives the full measure of his anxiety:

"Mr. Eliot, of Fairfield, is this moment arrived, on his way to Boston. He read us a letter from the Dr., his father, dated yesterday sennight, being Sunday. The Dr.'s description of the melancholy of the town is enough to melt a stone. The trials of that unhappy and devoted people are likely to be severe indeed. God grant that the furnace of affliction may refine them. God grant that they may be relieved from their present distress.

"It is arrogance and presumption, in human sagacity, to pretend to penetrate far into the designs of Heaven. The most perfect reverence and resignation becomes us, but I cannot help depending upon this, that the present dreadful calamity of that beloved town is intended to bind the colonies together in more indissoluble bonds, and to animate their exertions at this great crisis in the affairs of mankind. It has this effect in a most remarkable degree, as far as I have yet seen or heard. It will

plead with all America with more irresistible persuasion than angels trumpet-tongued.

"In a cause which interests the whole globe, at
a time when my friends and country are in such
keen distress, I am scarcely ever interrupted in the
least degree by apprehensions for my personal
safety. I am often concerned for you and our dear
babes, surrounded, as you are, by people who are
too timorous and too much susceptible of alarms.
Many fears and jealousies and imaginary dangers
will be suggested to you, but I hope you will not
be impressed by them. In case of real danger, of
which you cannot fail to have previous intimations,
fly to the woods with our children. Give my tenderest love to them, and to all."

"Fly to the woods with our children"! The
words tell only too plainly how terrible was the
danger the writer apprehended. The woods were
—or at any moment might be—full of prowling
savages, from whom no mercy could be expected;
yet John Adams would choose to run this risk
rather than others that threatened, or seemed to
threaten, his dear ones. One feels through all the
years the thrill of his anxiety.

"For the space of twelve months," says John
Quincy Adams, "my mother with her infant chil-

dren dwelt liable every hour of the day and night
to be butchered in cold blood or taken into Boston
as hostages by any foraging or marauding detach-
ment of men like that actually sent forth on the
19th of April to capture John Hancock and Samuel Adams, on their way to attend the Continental
Congress at Philadelphia. My father was separated
from his family on his way to attend the same congress, and then my mother and her children lived
in unintermitted danger of being consumed with
them all in a conflagration kindled by a torch in
the same hands which on the 17th of June lighted
the fires of Charlestown."

Abigail, in Braintree, no longer "calm and
happy," laments over the sufferings of her friends
and former neighbors.

"5 May, 1775.

"The distresses of the inhabitants of Boston are
beyond the power of language to describe; there
are but very few who are permitted to come out
in a day; they delay giving passes, make them wait
from hour to hour, and their counsels are not two
hours alike. One day, they shall come out with
their effects; the next day, merchandise is not effects. One day, their household furniture is to

come out; the next, only wearing apparel; the next, Pharaoh's heart is hardened, and he refuseth to hearken to them, and will not let the people go. May their deliverance be wrought out for them, as it was for the children of Israel. I do not mean by miracles, but by the interposition of Heaven in their favor. They have taken a list of all those who they suppose were concerned in watching the tea, and every other person whom they call obnoxious, and they and their effects are to suffer destruction.

"Yours, PORTIA."

"24 May, 1775.

"I suppose you have had a formidable account of the alarm we had last Sunday morning. When I rose, about six o'clock, I was told that the drums had been some time beating, and that three alarm guns were fired; that Weymouth bell had been ringing, and Mr. Weld's was then ringing. I immediately sent off an express to know the occasion, and found the whole town in confusion. Three sloops and one cutter had come out and dropped anchor just below Great Hill. It was difficult to tell their designs; some supposed they were coming to Germantown, others to Weymouth; people, women, children, from the iron-works, came flocking down this way; every woman and child driven off from below my father's; my father's family flying. The Dr. is in great distress, as you may well imagine, for my aunt had her bed thrown into a cart, into which she got herself, and ordered the boy to drive her to Bridgewater, which he did. The report was to them that three hundred British had landed, and were upon their march up into town. The alarm flew like lightning, and men from all parts came flocking down, till two thousand were collected. But it seems their expedition was to Grape Island for Levett's hay. There it was impossible to reach them for want of boats; but the sight of so many people, and the firing at them, prevented their getting more than three tons of hay, though they had carted much more down to the water. At last a lighter was mustered, and a sloop from Hingham, which had six port-holes. Our men eagerly jumped on board, and put off for the Island. As soon as they perceived it, they decamped. Our people landed upon the island, and in an instant set fire to the hay, which, with the barn, was soon consumed,— about eighty tons, it is said. We expect soon to be in continual alarms, till something decisive takes place. . . . Our house has been, upon this alarm, in the same scene of confusion that it was upon the former.   Soldiers coming in for a lodging, for breakfast, for supper, for drink, etc.   Sometimes refugees from Boston, tired and fatigued, seek an asylum for a day, a night, a week.   You can hardly imagine how we live; yet,—

> To the houseless child of want,
>   Our doors are open still;
> And though our portions are but scant,
>   We give them with good will.

"My best wishes attend you, both for your health and happiness, and that you may be directed into the wisest and best measures for our safety and the security of our posterity.   I wish you were nearer to us; we know not what a day will bring forth, nor what distress one hour may throw us into.   Hitherto, I have been able to maintain a calmness and presence of mind, and hope I shall, let the exigency of the time be what it will. . . ."

"Weymouth, 15 June, 1775.

"I sat down to write to you on Monday, but really could not compose myself sufficiently; the anxiety I suffered from not hearing one syllable from you for more than five weeks, and the new distress arising from the arrival of recruits, agi-

tated me more than I have been since the never-
to-be-forgotten 14th of April. I have been much
revived by receiving two letters from you last
night. . . .

"We cannot but consider the great distance you
are from us as a very great misfortune, when our
critical situation renders it necessary to hear from
you every week, and will be more and more so, as
difficulties arise. We now expect our seacoast rav-
aged; perhaps the very next letter I write will inform you that I am driven away from our yet quiet
cottage. Necessity will oblige Gage to take some
desperate steps. We are told for truth that he is
now eight thousand strong. We live in continual
expectations of alarms. Courage I know we have
in abundance; conduct I hope we shall not want;
but powder,—where shall we get a sufficient supply?
I wish we may not fail there. Every town is filled
with the distressed inhabitants of Boston. Our
house [1] among others is deserted, and by this time,
like enough, made use of as a barrack. . . .

"I have a request to make of you; something like
the barrel of sand, I suppose you will think it, but
really of much more importance to me. It is, that
you would send out Mr. Bass, and purchase me a

[1] I. e., their house in Boston.

bundle of pins and put them in your trunk for me.
The cry for pins is so great that what I used to buy
for seven shillings and sixpence are now twenty
shillings, and not to be had for that.   A bundle
contains six thousand, for which I used to give a
dollar; but if you can procure them for fifty shillings, or three pounds (ten dollars), pray let me
have them.

"I am, with the tenderest regard,

"Your PORTIA."

On June 17th, John Adams writes:

"I can now inform you that the Congress have
made choice of the modest and virtuous, the amiable, generous and brave George Washington, Es-
quire, to be General of the American army, and
that he is to repair, as soon as possible, to the camp
before Boston.   This announcement will have a
great effect in cementing and securing the union of
these colonies.   The continent is really in earnest,
in defending the country.   They have voted ten
companies of riflemen to be sent from Pennsylvania,
Maryland and Virginia, to join the army before
Boston.   These are an excellent species of light infantry.   They use a peculiar kind of musket, called
a rifle.   It has circular or—(word effaced in manu-
script) grooves within the barrel, and carries a ball

with great exactness to great distances. They are the most accurate marksmen in the world. . . .

"America is a great, unwieldy body. Its progress must be slow. It is like a large fleet sailing under convoy. The fleetest sailors must wait for the dullest and slowest. Like a coach and six, the swiftest horses must be slackened, and the slowest quickened, that all may keep an even pace. . . ."

Mr. Adams little thought that even while he wrote, the cannon were roaring on Bunker Hill, and that on its slopes,

> In their ragged regimentals
> Stood the old Continentals,
>   Yielding not,
> When the grenadiers were lunging,
> And like hail fell the plunging
>   Cannon-shot.

Abigail Adams heard the cannon, and taking her seven-year-old Johnny with her, mounted Penn's Hill, at the foot of which the house stood. Standing there, mother and son saw with terror the smoke of burning Charlestown, listened with beating hearts to the beating drums and roaring cannon. The boy never forgot that hour. Long after he would tell of it, and of his mother's deep distress on hearing of the death of Warren.

The news of Bunker Hill reached Philadelphia on June 22d: on the 27th, John Adams writes:

"This moment received two letters from you. Courage, my dear. We shall be supported in life or comforted in death. I rejoice that my country-men behaved so bravely, though not so skilfully conducted as I could wish. I hope this defeat will be remedied by the new modeling of the army.

"My love everywhere."

This brief letter crossed one from Abigail, dated June 25th.

"I hear that General Howe said that the battle upon the Plains of Abram was but a bauble to this. When we consider all the circumstances attending this action, we stand astonished that our people were not all cut off. They had but one hundred feet in-trenched, the number who were engaged did not ex-ceed eight hundred, and they with not half ammu-nition enough; the reinforcement not able to get to them seasonably. The tide was up, and high, so that their floating batteries came upon each side of the causeway, and their row-galleys kept a con-tinual fire. Added to this, the fire from Copp's Hill, and from the ships; the town in flames, all around them, and the heat from the flames so intense as scarcely to be borne; the day one of the hottest we have had this season, and the wind blowing the smoke in their faces,—only figure to yourself all these circumstances, and then consider that we do not count sixty men lost. My heart overflows at the recollection.

"We live in continual expectation of hostilities. Scarcely a day that does not produce some; but, like good Nehemiah, having made our prayer unto God, and set the people with their swords, their spears, and their bows, we will say unto them, 'Be ye not afraid of them; remember the Lord, who is great and terrible, and fight for your brethren, your sons, and your daughters, your wives and your houses.'

"I have just received yours of the 17th of June, in seven days only; every line from that far country is precious. . . . O North, may the groans and cries of the injured and oppressed harrow up thy soul!"

While she wrote, Washington was on the march. He reached Watertown on July 2d, and on the 3d, standing under the tree which still (1917) marks the spot, he took command of the Continental Army.

On July 5th, she writes:

"I should have been more particular, but I thought you knew everything that passed here. The present state of the inhabitants of Boston is that of the most abject slaves, under the most cruel and despotic tyrants. Among many instances I could mention, let me relate one. Upon the 17th of June, printed handbills were posted up at the corners of the streets, and upon houses, forbidding any inhabitants to go upon their houses, or upon any eminence, on pain of death; the inhabitants dared not to look out of their houses, nor to be heard or seen to ask a question. Our prisoners were brought over to the Long Wharf, and there lay all night, without any care of their wounds, or any resting-place but the pavements, until the next day, when they exchanged it for the jail, since which we hear they are civilly treated. Their living cannot be good, as they can have no fresh provisions; their beef, we hear, is all gone, and their wounded men die very fast, so that they have a report that the bullets were poisoned. Fish they cannot have, they have rendered it so difficult to procure; and the admiral is such a villain as to oblige every fishing schooner to pay a dollar every time it goes out. The money that has been paid for passes is incredible. Some have given ten, twenty, thirty, and forty dollars, to get out with a small proportion of their things. It is reported and believed that they have taken up a number of persons and committed them to jail, we know not for what in particular. Master Lovell is confined in the dungeon; a son of Mr. Edes is in jail, and one Wiburt, a ship-carpenter, is now upon trial for his life. God alone knows to what length these wretches will go, and will, I hope, restrain their malice.

"I would not have you distressed about me. Danger, they say, makes people valiant. Hitherto I have been distressed, but not dismayed. I have felt for my country and her sons. I have bled with them and for them. Not all the havoc and devastation they have made has wounded me like the death of Warren. We want him in the Senate; we want him in his profession; we want him in the field. We mourn for the citizen, the senator, the physician, and the warrior. May we have others raised up in his room. . . .

"I hope we shall not now have famine added to war. Grain, grain is what we want here. Meat we have enough, and to spare. Pray don't let Bass forget my pins. Hardwick has applied to me for Mr. Bass to get him a hundred of needles, number six, to carry on his stocking weaving. We shall very soon have no coffee, nor sugar, nor pepper, here; but whortleberries and milk we are not obliged to commerce for. . . . Good night. With thought of thee do I close my eyes. Angels guard and protect thee; and may a safe return ere long bless thy

"Portia."

Dr. Lovell, who was "confined in the dungeon," was the Boston schoolmaster, a worthy man, and a stout patriot. The story is told that on the morning of the 19th of April, 1775, sitting at his desk in the schoolroom, he saw Earl Percy march by with his troops, on the way to Lexington. The master closed his book.

"War's begun, school's done!" he said. "*Deponite libros.*"

On the 16th, Abigail writes again:

"The appointment of the generals Washington and Lee gives universal satisfaction. The people have the highest opinion of Lee's abilities, but you know the continuation of the popular breath depends much upon favorable events. I had the pleasure of seeing both the generals and their aids-decamp soon after their arrival, and of being personally made known to them. . . .

"I was struck with General Washington. You had prepared me to entertain a favorable opinion of him, but I thought the half was not told me. Dignity with ease and complacency, the gentleman

and the soldier, look agreeably blended in him.
Modesty marks every line and feature of his face.
These lines of Dryden instantly occurred to me:—

> Mark his majestic fabric; he's a temple
> Sacred by birth, and built by hands divine;
> His soul's the deity that lodges there,
> Nor is the pile unworthy of the god.

"General Lee looks like a careless, hardy veteran,
and by his appearance brought to my mind his name-
sake, Charles the Twelfth, of Sweden. The elegance of his pen far exceeds that of his person. . . .

"As to intelligence from Boston, it is but very
seldom we are able to collect anything that may be
relied on; and to report the vague flying rumors
would be endless. I heard yesterday, by one Mr.
Roulstone, a goldsmith, who got out in a fishing
schooner, that their distress increased upon them
fast. Their beef is all spent; their malt and cider
all gone. All the fresh provisions they can procure
they are obliged to give to the sick and wounded.
Thirteen of our men who were in jail, and were
wounded at the battle of Charlestown, were dead.
No man dared now to be seen talking to his friend
in the street. They were obliged to be within,
every evening, at ten o'clock, according to martial

law; nor could any inhabitants walk any street in town after that time, without a pass from Gage. . . .

"Every article in the West India way is very scarce and dear. In six weeks we shall not be able to purchase any article of the kind. I wish you would let Bass get me one pound of pepper and two yards of black calamanco for shoes. I cannot wear leather, if I go barefoot. Bass may make a fine profit if he lays in a stock for himself. You can hardly imagine how much we want many common small articles which are not manufactured amongst ourselves; but we will have them in time; not one pin to be purchased for love or money. I wish you would convey me a thousand by any friend traveling this way. It is very provoking to have such a plenty so near us, but, Tantalus-like, not to be able to touch. I should have been glad to have laid in a small stock of the West India articles, but I cannot get one copper; no person thinks of paying anything, and I do not choose to run in debt. I endeavor to live in the most frugal manner possible, but I am many times distressed."

"This is the 25th of July. Gage has not made any attempt to march out since the battle of Charlestown. Our army is restless, and wish to be doing something to rid themselves and the land of the vermin and locusts which infest it. Since I wrote you last, the companies stationed upon the coast, both in this town, Weymouth, and Hingham, were ordered to Nantasket, to reap and bring off the grain, which they accomplished, all except a field or two which was not ripe; and having whaleboats, they undertook to go to the Lighthouse and set fire to it, which they effected in open day, and in fair sight of several men-of-war. Upon their return, came down upon them eight barges, one cutter, and one schooner, all in battle-array, and poured whole broadsides upon them; but our men all reached the shore, and not one life lost, two only slightly wounded in their legs. They marched up a hill, and drew into order in hopes the marines would land; but they chose rather to return without a land engagement, though 'tis thought they will burn the town down as soon as our forces leave it. I had this account from Captain Vinton, who with his company, were there. These little skirmishes seem trifling, but they serve to inure our men, and harden them to danger. I hear the rebels are very wroth at the destruction of the Lighthouse.

"There has been an offer from Gage to send the poor of Boston to Salem, by water, but not complied with on our part; they returned for answer, they would receive them upon the lines. Dr. Tufts saw a letter from Deacon Newall, in which he mentions the death of John Cotton; he says it is very sickly in town. Every fishing vessel is now obliged to enter and clear out, as though she was going a foreign voyage. No inhabitant is suffered to partake, but obliged to wait till the army is supplied, and then, if one [fish] remains, they are allowed to purchase it. An order has been given out in town that no person shall be seen to wipe his face with a white handkerchief. The reason I hear is, that it is a signal of mutiny. General Burgoyne lives in Mr. Sam Quincy's house. A lady, who lived opposite, says she saw raw meat cut and hacked upon her mahogany tables, and her superb damask curtains and cushions exposed to the rain, as if they were of no value. . . ."

Up to this time, Mrs. Adams had only the sorrows of her neighbors to chronicle, but now her own turn was come. A violent epidemic of dysentery broke out in the surrounding country, and "calm, happy Braintree" was calm no longer. One after another of the family sickened; one of the servants first, Isaac, ("there was no resting-place in the house, for his terrible groans!") Mrs. Adams

herself was the next, and she was sorely tempted
to send for her husband, who was then but a few
days on his journey back to Philadelphia.

"I suffered greatly between my inclination to have
you return, and my fear of sending lest you should
be a partaker of the common calamity." . . . "Our
little Tommy was the next, and he lies very ill now.
. . . Our house is a hospital in every part; and
what with my own weakness and distress of mind
for my family, I have been unhappy enough. And
such is the distress of the neighborhood that I can
scarely find a well person to assist in looking after
the sick. . . . So sickly and so mortal a time the
oldest man does not remember. . . . As to politics, I know nothing about them. The distresses
of my own family are so great that I have not
thought of them. . . ."

One of the maids died; the others recovered,
though Tommy, who had been a "hearty, hale, corn-
fed boy," was now "entirely stripped of the hardy,
robust countenance, as well as of all the flesh he
had, save what remains for to keep his bones together." In October, Abigail's mother, after visiting a soldier home from the army on sick leave,
was stricken by the pestilence and died. This was
a heavy blow, and the daughter's heart cried out

to her absent mate. "Have pity on me, O thou my beloved, for the hand of God presseth me sore."

The letter which begins thus would move any heart even at this distance of time: to John Adams, it brought deep distress. The loving husband and father would fain take horse and ride post haste to Braintree; the steadfast patriot must remain at his post. All he could do was to write her frequently and as cheerfully as might be.

"I will never," he assures her on December third, "come here again without you, if I can persuade you to come with me. Whom God has joined together ought not to be put asunder so long, with their own consent. We will bring master Johnny with us; you and he shall have the small-pox here, and we will be as happy as Mr. Hancock and his lady. Thank Abby and John for their letters, and kiss Charles and Tom for me. John writes like a hero, glowing with ardor for his country and burning with indignation against her enemies. . . ."

Now and then, but rarely, he tried to amuse her with a story.

"A few days ago, in company with Dr. Zubly, somebody said there was nobody on our side but the Almighty. The Doctor, who is a native of Switzerland, and speaks but broken English, quickly replied, 'Dat is enough! Dat is enough!' And turning to me says he, 'It puts me in mind of a fellow who once said, "The Catholics have on their side the Pope, and the King of France, and the King of Spain, and the King of Sardinia, and the King of Poland, and the Emperor of Germany, etc., etc., etc.: but as to these poor devils the Protestants, they have nothing on their side but God Almighty." ' "

CHAPTER VI

BOSTON BLOCKADE

WHILE John and Abigail were writing their letters in Philadelphia and Braintree, Boston town was undergoing a winter of discontent indeed. Ever since Bunker Hill and the burning of Charlestown, the British troops had occupied the town, while Washington and his army lay encamped in Cambridge and on Dorchester Heights, west of the city. In October, the British command was transferred from General Gage to General Howe, who proved a more energetic commander. He burned Falmouth (now Portland), and threatened many other places. After the burning of Charlestown, Franklin wrote:

"Britain must certainly be distracted. No tradesman out of Bedlam ever thought of increasing the number of his customers by knocking them on the head, or of enabling them to pay their debts by burning their houses. It has been with difficulty that we have carried another humble Petition to the

Among the clergymen was one with whose name I have a pleasant association: the Reverend Mather Byles, pastor of Hollis Street Church. This gentleman was a merry, as well as a devout person; full of quips and cranks, and not always lacking in wanton wiles. John Adams quotes him as saying, when first the British troops occupied Boston, that "our grievances would now be red-dressed!" But my own thought of Mr. Byles recalls a story often told by my mother, which she may have heard in childhood from her grandfather, the old Revolutionary Colonel. It tells how one night the Reverend Mather, returning home very late, passed by the house of a man whom he greatly disliked. A sudden thought struck him; he went up the steps and began to beat and bang on the door and halloo at the top of his lungs. After some delay, the night-capped head of his neighbor was thrust out of the window, demanding what was to do at this time o' night.

"Have you lost a penknife?" asked Mr. Byles.

"No! Have you found one?"

"No, but I feel as if I should any minute!"

Exeunt both parties, one chuckling, the other swearing.

The Tories, rich, prosperous, and loyal to King George, were ready enough to help the officers in

making merry.   There were sleighing parties, riding
parties, parties of every description: no doubt the
Tory maidens found the winter a very gay one.
Faneuil Hall was turned into a theatre, and General Burgoyne wrote plays for it.   A performance
of "Zara" was a brilliant success.   After another
performance, a farce called "Boston Blockade," a
"Vaudevil" was to be sung by the characters, of
which the following is a part:

Ye Critics, who wait for an End of the Scene,
T' accept it with Praise or dismiss it with Spleen;
Your Candor we ask and demand your Applause,
If not for our Action, at least for our Cause.
'Tis our Aim by Amusement thus chearful and gay,
To wile a few Hours of Winter away:
While we rest on our arms, call the Arts to our Aid,
And be merry in spite of the BOSTON BLOCKADE.

Ye tarbarrel'd Lawgivers, yankified Prigs,
Who are Tyrants in Custom, yet call yourselves Whigs;
In return for the Favors you've lavish'd on me,
May I see you all hanged upon *Liberty Tree*.
Meantime take Example; decease from Attack;
You're as weak under Arms as I'm weak in my Back,
In War and in Love we alike are betrayed,
And alike are the laughter of BOSTON BLOCKADE.

Come round then, ye Comrades of Honour and Truth,
Experienc'd Age and high-spirited Youth;
With Drum and with Fife make the Chorus more shrill.
And echo shall waft it to WASHINGTON'S Hill.

All brave BRITISH Hearts shall beat Time while we
  sing,
Due Force to our Arms, and Long Life to the King.
To the Honour of both be our Banners display'd,
And a glorious End to the BOSTON BLOCKADE.

As it turned out, the audience had not the pleasure of listening to these polished verses. The performance was in full swing; a comic actor held the
stage, mimicking General Washington and holding
him up to ridicule, when a sergeant rushed on the
stage, crying, "The Yankees are attacking the works
on Bunker Hill!"

The audience, supposing this to be part of the
play, laughed and applauded: a happy thought! a
capital touch! What were their feelings when the
senior officer present rose and called, "Officers to
their posts!" The assembly broke up in disorder.
The officers summoned their men and hastened to
Bunker Hill, where they arrived too late! Major
Knowlton, who had fought so bravely in the battle
of June 17th, had paid a second visit to the hill,
burned some buildings and carried off several prisoners.

Meanwhile the Tory ladies, deprived of their gal-
lant red-coated escorts, scuttled home as best they
might through the dark, crooked streets, and their

patriot sisters, who had refused to go to the entertainment, made merry over the episode for days afterward.

To lovers of Hawthorne, this story might well be followed by that wonderful tale of "Howe's Masquerade,"[2] which used to thrill me as a child, and which I cannot even now read unmoved. If not true in actual fact, it gives with absolute truth the Spirit of Seventy-Six.

The winter was a mild one: all too mild for Washington. He was eager to cross the ice on the Back Bay and attack the town; but the ice would not bear. Week by week he watched and tested it; all in vain. It was not till February, that "strong little month," that the real cold came. "When the days begin to lengthen, the cold begins to strengthen." Day followed day of keen, dry cold; night by night the ice "made," till a floor of crystal, solid as rock, lay about the peninsula of Boston. Washington called a council of war and urged an assault on the town. Alas! his field officers demurred, shook their heads, would none of it. Reluctantly he abandoned the plan, and determined to seize instead Dorchester Heights and Noddle's Island (East Boston).

[2] "Twice-Told Tales." Nathaniel Hawthorne.

On March 2d, Abigail Adams writes to her husband:

"I have been kept in a continual state of anxiety and expectation ever since you left me. It has been said 'tomorrow' and 'tomorrow,' for this month, but when the dreadful tomorrow will be, I know not. But hark! The house this instant shakes with the roar of cannon. I have been to the door, and find it is a cannonade from our army. Orders, I find, are come for all the remaining militia to repair to the lines Monday night by twelve oclock. No sleep for me tonight. And if I cannot sleep, who have no guilt upon my soul with regard to this cause, how shall the miserable wretches who have been the procurers of this dreadful scene, and those who are to be the actors, lie down with the load of guilt upon their souls?"

The story continues through the following days.

Sunday evening.

"I went to bed after twelve, but got no rest; the cannon continued firing, and my heart beat pace with them all night. We have had a pretty quiet day, but what tomorrow will bring forth, God only knows."

"Monday evening. Tolerably quiet. Today the

militia have all mustered, with three days' pro-
vision, and are all marched by three o'clock this
afternoon, though their notice was no longer ago
than eight o'clock Saturday. And now we have
scarcely a man, but our regular guards, either in
Weymouth, Hingham, Braintree, or Milton, and the
militia from the more remote towns are called in
as seacoast guards. Can you form to yourself an
idea of our sensations?

"I have just returned from Penn's Hill, where I
have been sitting to hear the amazing roar of cannon, and from whence I could see every shell which
was thrown. The sound, I think, is one of the
grandest in nature, and is of the true species of the
sublime. 'Tis now an incessant roar; but oh! the
fatal ideas which are connected with the sound!
How many of our dear countrymen must fall!

"Tuesday morning. I went to bed about twelve,
and rose again a little after one. I could no more
sleep than if I had been in the engagement; the rat-
tling of the windows, the jar of the house, the continual roar of twenty-four pounders, and the burst-
ing of shells, give us such ideas, and realize a scene
to us of which we could form scarcely any concep-
tion. About six, this morning, all was quiet. I
rejoiced in a few hours' calm. I hear we got pos-

session of Dorchester Hill last night; four thousand men upon it today; lost but one man. The ships are all drawn round the town. Tonight we shall realize a more terrible scene still. I sometimes think I cannot stand it. I wish myself with you, out of hearing, as I cannot assist them. I hope to give you joy of Boston, even if it is in ruins, before I send this away. I am too much agitated to write as I ought, and languid for want of rest.

"Thursday. All my anxiety and distress is at present at an end. I feel disappointed. This day our militia are all returning, without effecting anything more than taking possession of Dorchester Hill. I hope it is wise and just, but, from all the muster and stir, I hoped and expected more important and decisive scenes. I would not have suffered all I have for two such hills. Ever since the taking of that, we have had a perfect calm; nor can I learn what effect it has had in Boston. I do not hear of one person's escaping since."

Abigail need not have suffered even this momentary discouragement, could she have foreseen the outcome of these hours of suspense. The cannonade which so shook the neighboring towns was ordered by Washington to divert the attention of the British, and to drown the noise of carts crossing the frozen ground: carts whose wheels were bound with straw, and before which the road was strewn with straw, still further to deaden the sound. General Thomas was moving from Roxbury to South Boston with twelve hundred men. Silently, under cover of the darkness, and later of a thick white fog, under shelter of that good thunder of the Cambridge guns, they marched; silently, they took their new stand, laid down their arms to take up pick-axe and spade. In the morning, when the fog lifted, the amazed British looked out on a row of formidable entrenchments on Dorchester Heights, just above their heads.

Great was the consternation. Howe summoned his officers, and prepared for a counter-attack; but Dame Nature, apparently in league with the patriots, responded with a furious storm which, lasting several days, made the action from Castle Island which he had planned impossible. During these days of storm, Washington was strengthening his defenses. Howe looked, and realized that the game was up. Others realized it too: the selectmen of Boston quietly intimated to him that if he left the town uninjured, his troops would be suffered to embark undisturbed. Washington gave no sign; waited, his powder dry, his matches burning. Nor did Howe answer the citizens in words; no words were needed for what he had to do. By daybreak on March 17th, the troops began to embark; by nine o'clock the last boat had put off. Boston was evacuated, and Washington and his Continentals entered the city.[3]

"The actors in the scene have vanished into deeper obscurity than even that wild Indian band who scattered the cargoes of the tea ships on the waves, and gained a place in history, yet left no names. But superstition, among other legends of this mansion, (the Province House) repeats the wondrous tale, that on the anniversary night of Britain's discomfiture the ghosts of the ancient governors of Massachusetts still glide through the portal of the Province House. And, last of all, comes a figure shrouded in a military cloak, tossing his clenched hands into the air, and stamping his ironshod boots upon the broad freestone steps, with a semblance of feverish despair, but without the sound of a foot-tramp." [4]

[3] Be it remembered that Washington did not remain in Boston, but anticipating Howe's attack on New York, was encamped in Brooklyn Heights by April: these movements ended the operations in New England. New York was the centre of the next campaign.

[4] "Legends of the Province House." Nathaniel Hawthorne.

CHAPTER VII

IN HAPPY BRAINTREE

WHAT was home life like, when Johnny and Abby Adams were little? It would be pleasant to see something of it in detail; if Mrs. Adams had only kept a diary! As it is, it is mostly by side-lights that we can get a glimpse of that Braintree home, so happy in itself, so shadowed, in the days of which I write, by the tremendous cloud of public events.

We know that Mrs. Adams spent some part of each day in writing letters; but we have to stop and think about the other things she did, some of them were so different from the things women do today. Take the spinning and weaving! A spinning wheel, for us, is a pretty, graceful article of furniture, very useful for *tableaux vivants* and the like; in the Adams household it was as constantly and inevitably used as our own sewing-machine. So was the loom, which is banished altogether from New Eng-

and homes, though in some parts of the South it is still in use. Mrs. Adams and her maids, Susie and Patty (poor Patty, who died that summer of 1775!), not only made, but spun and wove, every article of clothing, every sheet, blanket, table-cloth, that the house afforded. The wool-wheel is a large clumsy affair, very different from the elegant little flax-wheel. You may still find it in some New England households. Some years ago, driving along a remote road, I came to a little brown house, so old and moss-covered that it seemed almost a part of the wood that surrounded it. I knocked, and hearing a cheery "Come in!" entered to find a neat kitchen, half filled by an enormous wheel, in front of which a little brownie of a woman was stepping back and forth, diligently spinning yarn. It was a pretty sight.

Thinking of this, and trying, as I am constantly doing, to link the new time to the old, I find myself calling up another picture, a scene on Boston Common in the year 1749, when a society, formed for promoting industry and frugality, publicly celebrated its fourth anniversary. "In the afternoon about three hundred young female spinsters, decently dressed, appeared on the Common at their spinning wheels. The wheels were placed regularly

in rows, and a female was seated at each wheel.
The weavers also appeared, cleanly dressed, in garments of their own weaving. One of them working at a loom on a stage was carried on men's shoulders, attended with music. An immense number
of spectators were present."

I wonder if Mrs. Adams and her maidens made
any "Bounty Coats." When Washington gathered
his army in May, 1775, there were no overcoats
for the men. The Provincial Congress "made a
demand on the people for thirteen thousand warm
coats to be ready for the soldiers by cold weather."
There were no factories then, remember : no steam-
power, no contractors, no anything—except the women and their wheels. All over the country, the
big wool-wheels began to fly, the shuttles sped back
and forth through the sounding looms. Every
town, every village, every lonely farmhouse, would
do its part; long before the appointed time, the coats
were ready. Inside each coat was sewed the name
of town and maker. Every soldier, volunteering
for eight months' service, was given one of these
coats as a bounty. We are told that "so highly
were these 'Bounty Coats' prized, that the heirs
of soldiers who were killed at Bunker Hill before
receiving their coats were given a sum of money

instead. The list of names of soldiers who then en-
listed is known to this day as the 'Coat Roll,' and
the names of the women who made the coats might
form another roll of honor."

I cannot be sure that one or more of these coats
came from the lean-to farmhouse in Braintree, but
I like .to think so, and certainly nothing is more
probable.

The women who refused to drink tea determined
also to do without imported dress materials. From
Massachusetts to South Carolina, the Daughters of
Liberty agreed to wear only homespun garments.
General Howe, finding "Linnen and Woollen Goods
much wanted by the Rebels," carried away with
him, when he evacuated Boston, all of such things
as he could lay hands on. He reckoned without
the spinners! In town and village, the Daughters
flocked together, bringing their flax-wheels with
them, sometimes to the number of sixty or seventy.
In Rowley, Massachusetts, "A number of thirty-
three respectable ladies of the town met at sunrise
with their wheels to spend the day at the house of
the Rev'd Jedidiah Jewell, in the laudable design of
a spinning match. At an hour before sunset, the
ladies there appearing neatly dressed, principally in
homespun, a polite and generous repast of Ameri-

can production was set for their entertainment. After which being present many spectators of both sexes, Mr. Jewell delivered a profitable discourse from Romans xii. 2: 'Not slothful in business, fervent in spirit, serving the Lord.' " [1]

There was always a text and a sermon for the spinners; a favorite text was from the Book of Exodus: "And all the women that were wise-hearted did spin with their hands." The women of Northboro, forty-four of them, spun two thousand, two hundred, twenty-three knots of linen and tow, and wove one linen sheet and two towels, all in one day!

This is amazing; but another record outdoes it: an extract from the diary of a young Connecticut girl, Abigail Foote, in this very year, 1775:

"Fix'd gown for Prude,—Mend Mother's Riding-hood,—spun short thread,—Fix'd two gowns for Walsh's girls,—Carded tow,—Spun linen,—Worked on Cheese-basket,—Hatchel'd flax with Hannah, we did 51 lbs. apiece,—Pleated and ironed,—Read a Sermon of Doddridge's,—Spooled a piece,—Milked the cows,—Spun linen, did 50 knots,—Made a Broom of Guinea wheat straw,—Spun thread to whiten,—Set a Red dye,—Had two scholars from

[1] "Social Life in Old New England."   Mary C. Crawford.

Mrs. Taylors,—I carded two pounds of whole wool
and felt Nationly,—Spun harness twine,—Scoured
the pewter."

One feels confident that Abby Adams had no
such record as this to show. She was an industrious and capable girl, but Mother Abigail would
see to it that her day was not *all* spent in household
work. There were lessons to learn and recite; the
daughter of John Adams must have a cultivated
mind, as well as skilful fingers. John went to Mr.
Thatcher's school, but for "Nabby" and the two
younger boys, "Mother" was the sole instructress.
Both parents were full of anxious care and thought
for the children's well-being. There is a beautiful
letter from Mr. Adams, written in April, 1776, in
which, after describing his multifarious labors, he
thus pours out his mind.

"What will come of this labor, time will discover. I shall get nothing by it, I believe, because
I never get anything by anything that I do. I am
sure the public or posterity ought to get something.
I believe my children will think I might as well have
thought and labored a little, night and day, for their
benefit. But I will not bear the reproaches of my
children. I will tell them that I studied and labored to procure a free constitution of government

for them to solace themselves under, and if they do
not prefer this to ample fortune, to ease and elegance, they are not my children, and I care not
what becomes of them. They shall live upon thin
diet, wear mean clothes, and work hard with cheerful hearts and free spirits, or they may be the children of the earth, or of no one, for me.

"John has genius, and so has Charles. Take
care that they don't go astray. Cultivate their
minds, inspire their little hearts, raise their wishes.
Fix their attention upon great and glorious objects.
Root out every little thing. Weed out every mean-
ness. Make them great and manly. Teach them to
scorn injustice, ingratitude, cowardice, and false-
hood. Let them revere nothing but religion, mor-
ality, and liberty.

"Abby and Tommy are not forgotten by me, although I did not mention them before. The first,
by reason of her sex, requires a different education
from the two I have mentioned. Of this, you are
the only judge. I want to send each of my little
pretty flock some present or other. I have walked
over this city twenty times, and gaped at every shop,
like a countryman, to find something, but could not.
Ask everyone of them what they would choose to
have, and write it to me in your next letter. From

this I shall judge of their taste and fancy and discretion."

Husband and wife are full of forebodings, yet have always a heartening word for each other.

"I have some thought," writes Mr. Adams, "of petitioning the General Court for leave to bring my family here. I am a lonely, forlorn creature here. . . . It is a cruel reflection, which very often comes across me, that I should be separated so far from those babes whose education and welfare lie so near my heart. But greater misfortunes than these must not divert us from superior duties.

"Your sentiments of the duties we owe to our country are such as become the best of women and the best of men. Among all the disappointments and perplexities which have fallen to my share in life, nothing has contributed so much to support my mind as the choice blessing of a wife whose capacity enabled her to comprehend, and whose pure virtue obliged her to approve, the views of her husband. This has been the cheering consolation of my heart in my most solitary, gloomy, and disconsolate hours. . . . I want to take a walk with you in the garden, to go over to the common, the plain, the meadow. I want to take Charles in one hand and Tom in the other, and walk with you, Abby on your

right hand and John upon my left, to view the corn
fields, the orchards, etc. . . ."

Shortly after this, on June 3d, Abigail writes:

"I wish to hear from you every opportunity,
though you say no more than that you are well. I
feel concerned lest your clothes should go to rags,
having nobody to take any care of you in your long
absence; and then, you have not with you a proper
change for the seasons. However, you must do the
best you can. I have a suit of homespun for you
whenever you return. I cannot avoid sometimes
repining that the gifts of fortune were not bestowed
upon us, that I might have enjoyed the happiness
of spending my days with my partner, but as it is,
I think it my duty to attend with frugality and
economy to our own private affairs; and if I cannot
add to our little substance, yet see to it that it is
not diminished. I should enjoy but little comfort in
a state of idleness and uselessness. Here I can
serve my partner, my family, and myself, and enjoy the satisfaction of your serving your country. . .

"Everything bears a very great price. The merchant complains of the farmer and the farmer of
the merchant,—both are extravagant. Living is
double what it was one year ago.

"I find you have licensed tea, but I am deter-

mined not to be a purchaser unless I can have it
at Congress price, and in that article the vendors
pay no regard to Congress, asking ten, eight, and
the lowest is seven and sixpence per pound. I should
like a little green, but they say there is none to be
had here. I only wish it for a medicine, as a relief to a nervous pain in my head to which I am
sometimes subject. Were it as plenty as ever, I
would not practice the use of it."

Beside spinning, weaving and making all the
clothing, Mrs. Adams and her maids must make
all the soap for the family; this was a regular part
of the housewife's duty, and a disagreeable part
it was.

"You inquire of me," she writes, "whether I am
making saltpetre. I have not yet attempted it, but
after soap-making believe I shall make the experiment. I find as much as I can do to manufacture
clothing for my family, which would else be naked."

Many women were making saltpetre for the gunpowder; let us hope they had fewer other necessary
occupations than Mrs. Adams.

Be sure that with all the plainer parts of house-
wifery, Abby was also instructed in its graces. We
can picture her sitting by her mother's side (Brother
Johnny, perhaps, reading aloud the while from

"Rollin's Ancient History," a work which he found entrancing) working at her sampler, or knitting a purse for Papa, far away, or mittens for her brothers. All the mittens and stockings, of course, were made at home as well as the clothes. Mitten knitting could be a fine art in those days. We read that one "young New Hampshire girl, using fine flaxen yarn, knit the whole alphabet and a verse of poetry into a pair of mittens!" Then there is the wonderful story of Nancy Peabody. How her brother, coming in from work at night, announced that he had lost his mittens. How Nancy ran to the garret for wool, carded and spun a big hank of yarn that night, soaked and scoured it next morning, and as soon as it was dry, sat down to knit. "In twenty-four hours from the time the brother announced his loss he had a fine new pair of double mittens." "I tell the tale as I've heard told."

Did Abby learn netting with all the rest? Doubtless sh: did. Lady Washington set the fashion, and netted so well and so industriously that all her family were proud of trimming their dresses with her work. Then there was quilting, a fine art indeed in those days, and the exquisite embroidery which we find in our grandmothers' cupboards, and over which we sigh partly in admiration, partly in compassion for the eyes which were so cruelly tried; and a dozen other niceties and exquisitenesses of needlework. To quote the advertisement of Mrs. Sarah Wilson, who kept a boarding-school for girls in Philadelphia:

"Young ladies may be educated in a genteel manner, and pains taken to teach them in regard to their behaviour, on reasonable terms. They may be taught all sorts fine needlework, viz., working on catgut or flowering muslin, sattin stitch, quince stitch, tent stitch, cross-stitch, open work, tambour, embroidering curtains or chairs, writing and cyphering. Likewise waxwork in all its several branches, never as yet particularly taught here; also how to take profiles in wax, to make wax flowers and fruits and pinbaskets."

Boston would not be behind Philadelphia in matters of high fashion.

In the Boston *News-Letter,* in August, 1716, we read:

"This is to give notice that at the House of Mr. George Brownell, late Schoolmaster in Hanover Street, Boston, are all sorts of Millinery Works done; making up Dresses and flowering of Muslin, making of furbelow'd Scarffs, and Quilting and cutting of Gentlewomen's Hair in the newest Fashion;

and also young Gentlewomen and children taught all sorts of fine works, as Feather-work, Filigre and Painting on Glass, Embroidering a new way, Turkey-work for Handkerchiefs two ways, fine new Fashion purses, flourishing and plain Work, and Dancing cheaper than was ever taught in Boston. Brocaded work for Handkerchiefs and short Aprons upon Muslin; artificial Flowers work'd with a needle."

And what did Abby Adams wear, say in 1776, when she was ten years old? Why, she wore a large hoop, and, I fear, very uncomfortable corsets, with a stiff board down the front; high-heeled shoes, and mitts reaching to her elbows, and a ruffled or embroidered apron. Of all this we may be tolerably sure, as it was the costume of the time. We may hope, however, Mrs. Adams being the sensible woman she was, that Abby did not suffer like Dolly Payne (afterward Dolly Madison), who went to school wearing "a white linen mask to keep every ray of sunshine from the complexion, a sunbonnet sewed on her head every morning by her careful mother, and long gloves covering the hands and arms."

When Nelly Custis was four years old, her stepfather, General Washington, ordered an outfit for her from England, "pack-thread stays, stiff coats of silk, masks, caps, bonnets, bibs, ruffles, necklaces, fans, silk and calamanco shoes, and leather pumps. There were also eight pairs of kid mitts and four pairs of gloves." Poor Nelly!

But to return to Abby Adams. One article of her winter costume has a personal interest for me, because it survived to my own time, and I suffered under, or rather *in* it, in my childhood. The pumpkin hood! It has genuine historical interest, for it dates back to the days of the unwarmed meeting-house, when a woman or a girl-child must wrap up her head, and smuggle in a hot brick or a hot stick for her feet, if she would keep alive through meeting. How ugly the thing was! Of clumsy oblong shape, coming well forward over the face; heavily quilted, an inch thick or so; knots of narrow ribbon or of worsted sticking up here and there; I detested it, thought it a hardship to be condemned to wear it, instead of being thankful for warm ears and a historic atmosphere. I think our pumpkin hoods were among the last to survive, and some of the other girls had already beauteous things called skating-caps, fitting the head closely, displaying pie-shaped sections of contrasting colors, gray and purple, blue and scarlet, knitted or crocheted, I forget

which. Looking back to the early Sixties, the skat-
ing-cap still seems among the greatly desirable
things of life.

Perhaps we have gone as far as we can in pictur-
ing little Abby Adams, who grew up an accomplished and charming young woman, and in due time
married, by curious coincidence, a Mr. Smith, thus
taking as a married woman her mother's maiden
name. Let us return to the elder Abigail.

Left alone to manage all affairs, household and
educational, it is not strange that her keen, alert
mind sought wider fields for exercise than home life
afforded. She thought for herself, and her thought
took a direction which now seems prophetic. No
doubt she was in merry mood when she wrote to
John on March 31st, 1776, yet there is a ring of
earnestness under the playfulness.

(Note that the Assembly of Virginia, roused by
the burning of Norfolk, had just voted to propose
to Congress "that the colonies be declared free and
independent"; and afterward the British flag had
been hauled down at Williamsburg and replaced by
a banner with thirteen stripes.)

"I long to hear," writes Abigail to her dearest
friend, "that you have declared an independency.
And, by the way, in the new code of laws which I

suppose it will be necessary for you to make, I desire you would remember the ladies and be more generous and favorable to them than your ancestors. Do not put such unlimited power into the hands of the husbands. Remember, all men would be tyrants if they could. If particular care and attention is not paid to the ladies, we are determined to foment a rebellion, and will not hold ourselves bound by any laws in which we have no voice or representation.

"That your sex are naturally tyrannical is a truth so thoroughly established as to admit of no dispute; but such of you as wish to be happy willingly give up the harsh title of master for the more tender and endearing one of friend. Why, then, not put it out of the power of the vicious and the lawless to use us with cruelty and indignity with impunity? Men of sense in all ages abhor those customs which treat us only as the vassals of your sex; regard us then as beings placed by Providence under your protection, and in imitation of the Supreme Being make use of that power only for our happiness."

Mr. Adams replies, in high amusement:

"As to your extraordinary code of laws, I cannot but laugh. We have been told that our struggle has loosened the bonds of government everywhere;

that children and apprentices were disobedient; that schools and colleges were grown turbulent; that Indians slighted their guardians, and negroes grew insolent to their masters. But your letter was the first intimation that another tribe, more numerous and powerful than all the rest, were grown discontented. This is rather too coarse a compliment, but you are so saucy, I won't blot it out. Depend upon it, we know better than to repeal our masculine systems. Although they are in full force, you know they are little more than theory. We dare not exert our power in its full latitude. We are obliged to go fair and softly, and, in practice, you know we are the subjects. We have only the name of masters, and rather than give up this, which would completely subject us to the despotism of the petticoat, I hope General Washington and all our brave heroes would fight; I am sure every good politician would plot, as long as he would against despotism, empire, monarchy, aristocracy, oligarchy, or ochlocracy. A fine story, indeed! I begin to think the ministry as deep as they are wicked. After stirring up Tories, land-jobbers, trimmers, bigots, Canadians, Indians, negroes, Hanoverians, Hessians, Russians, Irish Roman Catholic, Scotch renegades, at last they have stimulated the——to demand new privileges and threaten to rebel."

Doubtless John thought this settled the question; but Abigail had the last word to say.

"I cannot say that I think you are very generous to the ladies; for, whilst you are proclaiming peace and good-will to men, emancipating all nations, you insist upon retaining an absolute power over wives. But you must remember that arbitrary power is, like most other things which are very hard, very liable to be broken; and, notwithstanding all your wise laws and maxims, we have it in our power, not only to free ourselves, but to subdue our masters, and, without violence, throw both your natural and legal authority at our feet:——

> Charm by accepting, by submitting sway,
> Yet have our humor most when we obey."

CHAPTER VIII

INDEPENDENCE AT LAST

WHILE John and Abigail were tilting merrily at each other, the days were hastening on, and the first great climax of American history was drawing near. We must turn to our histories for the account of those June days in Philadelphia, when "the child Independence" was making his magical growth to manhood; when it was coming to be finally realized that "the country was not only ripe for independence, but was in danger of becoming rotten for want of it"; when the notable Committee of Five was appointed, charged with the duty of preparing a Declaration of the Independence of the thirteen colonies. Everyone knows their names: Roger Sherman, Robert Livingston, Benjamin Franklin, John Adams, Thomas Jefferson. Everyone knows that Jefferson wrote the Declaration; yet Adams, it was said, stood forth as "the Atlas of Independence," bearing on his shoulders the main burden of the tremendous decision.

We must read of it in his own words of solemn rejoicing:

"Yesterday, the greatest question was decided which ever was debated in America, and a greater, perhaps, never was nor will be decided among men. A Resolution was passed without one dissenting colony 'that these United Colonies are, and of right ought to be, free and independent States, and as such they have, and of right ought to have, full power to make war, conclude peace, establish commerce, and to do all other acts and things which other States may rightfully do.' You will see, in a few days, a Declaration setting forth the causes which have impelled us to this mighty revolution, and the reasons which will justify it in the sight of God and man. A plan of confederation will be taken up in a few days. . . .

"The second day of July, 1776, will be the most memorable epocha in the history of America. I am apt to believe that it will be celebrated by succeeding generations as the great anniversary festival. It ought to be commemorated as the day of deliverance, by solemn acts of devotion to God Almighty. It ought to be solemnized with pomp and parade, with shows, games, sports, guns, bells, bonfires, and illuminations, from one end of this continent to the other, from this time forward forevermore.

"You will think me transported with enthusiasm, but I am not. I am well aware of the toil and blood and treasure that it will cost us to maintain this Declaration and support and defend these States. Yet, through all the gloom, I can see the rays of ravishing light and glory. I can see that the end is more than worth all the means. And that posterity will triumph in that day's transaction, even although we should rue it, which I trust in God we shall not."

We celebrate the Fourth of July, the day upon which the form of the Declaration of Independence was agreed to, instead of the second, when it was determined upon by Congress. It matters little; these words of John Adams' shine like a halo round our Independence Day. May it ever be solemnized as he would have it, "from this time forward forevermore."

We can fancy the feelings of the faithful and loving wife as she read these words, which no American can ever read unmoved. We can see the tears rise to her bright dark eyes, tears of love and pride and trust unspeakable. We can see her gathering the children around her, Abby and John, Charles and even little Tommy, and reading the letter out to them in faltering but exultant tones. Yes, and we can see young John's head flung up, see his dark eyes, so like his mother's, brighten responsive, see, almost, the high beating of his answering heart. It was their great moment; we are glad to share in it, even a little.

Yet Abigail's reply is sober and discreet, like herself. She writes:

"By yesterday's post I received two letters dated 3d and 4th of July, and though your letters never fail to give me pleasure, be the subject what it will, yet it was greatly heightened by the prospect of the future happiness and glory of our country. Nor am I a little gratified when I reflect that a person so nearly connected with me has had the honor of being a principal actor in laying a foundation for its future greatness.

"May the foundation of our new Constitution be Justice, Truth, Righteousness! Like the wise man's house, may it be founded upon these rocks, and then neither storm nor tempests will overthrow it!"

And again on the 21st:

"Last Thursday, after hearing a very good sermon, I went with the multitude into King Street

[Boston] to hear the Proclamation for Independence read and proclaimed. Some field-pieces with the train were brought there. The troops appeared under arms, and all the inhabitants assembled there (the small-pox prevented many thousands from the country), when Colonel Crafts read from the balcony of the State House the proclamation. Great attention was given to every word. As soon as he ended, the cry from the balcony was, 'God save our American States,' and then three cheers which rent the air. The bells rang, the privateers fired, the forts and batteries, the cannon were discharged, the platoons followed, and every face appeared joyful. Mr. Bowdoin then gave a sentiment, 'Stability and perpetuity to American independence.' After dinner, the King's Arms were taken down from the State House, and every vestige of him from every place in which it appeared, and burnt in King Street. Thus ends royal authority in this State. And all the people shall say Amen."

Meantime a foe appeared far more terrible than any who wore a red coat, though he bore the same color; a foe whose little scarlet flag still carries terror to the heart, shorn as he is today of half his power.

The letters of this year are full of allusion to

the small-pox; in fact, a fearful epidemic was raging. Mr. Adams writes in June:

"The small-pox! the small-pox! what shall we do with it? I could almost wish that an inoculating hospital was opened in every town in New England. It is some small consolation that the scoundrel savages have taken a large dose of it. They plundered the baggage and stripped off the clothes of our men who had the small-pox out full upon them at the Cedars."

Vaccination was not yet, but careful people were hastening to be inoculated, all the country over. Mrs. Adams took all the children into Boston for this purpose, and a miserable time they had of it. Her eyes were much affected, and for some days she could not write. Mr. Adams, receiving no letters, on July 20th grew anxious:

"This has been a dull day to me. I waited the arrival of the post with much solicitude and impatience, but his arrival made me more solicitous still. 'To be left at the Post Office,' in your handwriting on the back of a few lines from the Dr. was all that I could learn of you and my little folks. If you were too busy to write, I hoped that some kind hand would have been found to let me know something about you. Do my friends think that I have been a politician so long as to have lost all feeling? Do they suppose I have forgotten my wife and children? Or are they so panic-struck with the loss of Canada as to be afraid to correspond with me? Or have they forgotten that you have a husband, and your children a father? What have I done, or omitted to do, that I should be thus forgotten and neglected in the most tender and affecting scene of my life? Don't mistake me. I don't blame you. Your time and thoughts must have been wholly taken up with your own and your family's situation and necessities; but twenty other persons might have informed me.

"I suppose that you intended to have run slyly through the small-pox with the family, without letting me know it, and then have sent me an account that you were all well. This might be a kind intention, and if the design had succeeded, would have made me very joyous. But the secret is out, and I am left to conjecture. But as the faculty have this distemper so much under command, I will flatter myself with the hope and expectation of soon hearing of your recovery."

A few days later he writes:

"How are you all this morning? Sick, weak, faint, in pain, or pretty well recovered? By this time, you are well acquainted with the small-pox. Pray, how do you like it?"

He had been inoculated himself, and knew all about it. He longed to send some comforting thing to his beloved, and fixed upon a canister of green tea, for which she had sometimes sighed, though she would not buy it. He sent the tea by a friend, Mr. Garry, "an old bachelor, and what is worse a politician." I must add, "what is worse still, an absent-minded person!" for he carried the tea to Mrs. *Samuel* Adams, who received it with great delight. Meantime, John Adams was flattering himself that his Abigail, amidst all her fatigues and distresses, was having "the poor relief of a dish of good tea." Mr. Garry returned to Philadelphia and Mr. Adams, meeting him, asked without a misgiving, "You delivered the tea?"

"Yes, to Mr. Samuel Adams' lady."

Poor John! he was so vexed that he ordered another canister and sent it by a surer hand. He bids his wife "send a card to Mrs. S. A., and let her know that the canister was intended for you, and she may send it you, if she chooses, as it was charged to me. It is amazingly dear; nothing less than forty shillings, lawful money, a pound."

Meantime Abigail was writing:

"The herbs you mention I never received. I was upon a visit to Mrs. S. Adams about a week after Mr. Garry returned, when she entertained me with a very fine dish of green tea. The scarcity of the article made me ask her where she got it. She replied that her *sweetheart* sent it to her by Mr. Garry. I said nothing, but thought my sweetheart might have been equally kind, considering the disease I was visited with, and that it was recommended as a bracer. A little after, you mentioned a couple of bundles sent. I supposed one of them might contain the article, but found they were letters. How Mr. Garry should make such a mistake I know not. I shall take the liberty of sending 'for what is left of it, though I suppose it is half gone, as it was very freely used. If you had mentioned a single word of it in your letter, I should have immediately found out the mistake."

Moral: Don't send "surprises" unless you are sure of the hand by which they are sent.

There are no letters between October, 1776, and January, 1777, which means that John Adams had a happy visit at home with his dear ones. A winter, too, of tremendous excitement, of breathless waiting for mails and despatches. We can see Mr. Adams in his arm chair, one January day, trying to read—let us say Xenophon! he would be good read-ing in those days—one eye on the book, the other out of window: Madam Abigail opposite, with Abby beside her, both at their tambour work.

"Isn't it time he was here?" says Mr. Adams for the tenth time; and he gets up and starts on para-sangs of his own up and down the room. Madam Abigail probably suggests patience, after the manner of women, but she looks out of window just as often as he does.

At last! at last comes the clatter of hoofs. The post-rider (only nine years old, and he has ridden all the way from Boston!) is here. The gate clicks, and Master Johnny's legs come flying up the path. He is waving a paper over his head; I don't know who gets to the door first, but I seem to see the Head of the Family tearing the despatch open in unstatesmanlike haste.

On Christmas night, he reads, General Washing-ton crossed the Delaware above Trenton, amid ice and snow, storm and tempest. He surprised the British camp, captured a thousand Hessians and car-ried them off with him to Pennsylvania.

Glory! glory! Stay! there is more. On the sec-ond of January, he was once more face to face with the British at Trenton, surrounded by them; they had him fast. "I have the old fox penned!" chuckles Cornwallis; "I'll bag him in the morning!"

But morning showed a row of empty earthworks, and the fox and his cubs well on their way to Princeton, where they fell upon another body of British, routed them in twenty minutes, and carried off three hundred of them, with much ammunition and arms, whereof they, to wit, fox and cubs, stood grievously in need.

This was the gist of the despatch; I do not pretend to give its wording. But fancy the effect of it, however worded, on the quiet Braintree household! John and Charles and even little Tommy, dancing up and down in their flapped waistcoats, shouting and huzzaing; Abby, very likely, shedding tears of happiness over her tambour frame; Father John striding up and down the room again, but now in different mood, probably declaiming lines from Horace in a voice that will not allow itself to tremble; Mother Abigail trying still to be Portia, and to pretend that she knows one end of the needle from the other. A pleasant picture indeed; and—who knows? Possibly not so far from the truth.

All the harder was it, amid all these great happenings, for Mr. Adams to mount and ride, leaving his dear ones to face the winter without him; but mount he must, and did.

He writes on his way back to Philadelphia:

"Present my affection in the tenderest manner to my little deserving daughter and my amiable sons. It was cruel parting this morning. My heart was most deeply affected, although I had the presence of mind to appear composed. May God Almighty's providence protect you, my dear, and all our little ones. My good genius, my guardian angel, whispers me that we shall see happier days, and that I shall live to enjoy the felicities of domestic life with her whom my heart esteems above all earthly blessings."

The war began to press heavily on New England housekeepers. Prices went steadily up, and the necessaries of life became hard to procure. Abigail writes in April, of 1777: "Indian corn at five shillings; rye, eleven and twelve shillings, but scarcely any to be had even at that price; beef, eight pence; veal, sixpence and eightpence; butter, one and sixpence; mutton, none; lamb, none; pork, none; cotton-wool, none; mean sugar, four pounds per hundred; molasses, none; New England rum, eight shillings per gallon; coffee, two and sixpence per pound; chocolate, three shillings."

She tells at the same time a curious story, of five Tories being carted out of town under the direction of "Joice junior," for refusing to take the paper money of the new Republic. "Joice junior" was a name which might be assumed by any patriot who wished to redress a grievance. He wore a horrible mask, and in this case "was mounted on horseback, with a red coat, a white wig, and a drawn sword, with drum and fife following. A concourse of people to the amount of five hundred followed. They proceeded as far as Roxbury, when he ordered the cart to be tipped up, then told them if they were ever caught in town again it should be at the expense of their lives. He then ordered his gang to return, which they did immediately without any disturbance."

In July, it is the women who take matters into their own hands.

"You must know," writes Abigail, "that there is a great scarcity of sugar and coffee, articles which the female part of the State is very loath to give up, especially whilst they consider the scarcity occasioned by the merchants having secreted a large quantity. There had been much rout and noise in the town for several weeks. Some stores had been opened by a number of people, and the coffee and sugar carried into the market and dealt out by pounds. It was rumored that an eminent, wealthy, stingy merchant (who is a bachelor) had a hogshead of coffee in his store, which he refused to sell to the committee under six shillings per pound. A number of females, some say a hundred, some say more, assembled with a cart and trucks, marched down to the warehouse, and demanded the keys, which he refused to deliver. Upon which one of them seized him by his neck, and tossed him into the cart. Upon his finding no quarter, he delivered the keys, when they tipped up the cart and discharged him; then opened the warehouse, hoisted out the coffee themselves, put it into the trucks, and drove off.

"It was reported that he had personal chastisement among them; but this, I believe, was not true. A large concourse of men stood amazed, silent spectators of the whole transaction."

This delighted John. "You have made me merry," he writes, "with the female frolic with the miser. But I hope the females will leave off their attachment to coffee. I assure you the best families in this place have left off, in a great measure, the use of West India goods. We must bring ourselves to live upon the produce of our own country.

What would I give for some of your cider? Milk has become the breakfast of many of the wealthiest and genteelest families here."

In August a report was spread that Howe's fleet was off Cape Ann. Boston took the alarm, and all was confusion, people packing up and carting out of town their household goods, military stores, in fact everything that was portable. Abigail writes:

"Not less than a thousand teams were employed on Friday and Saturday; and, to their shame be it told, not a small trunk would they carry under eight dollars, and many of them, I am told, asked a hundred dollars a load; for carting a hogshead of molasses eight miles, thirty dollars. O human nature! or rather O inhuman nature! what art thou? The report of the fleet's being seen off Cape Ann Friday night gave me the alarm and though pretty weak, I set about packing up my things, and on Saturday removed a load.

"When I looked around me and beheld the bounties of Heaven so liberally bestowed, in fine fields of corn, grass, flax, and English grain, and thought it might soon become a prey to these merciless ravagers, our habitations laid waste, and if our flight preserved our lives, we must return to barren fields, empty barns, and desolate habitations, if any we find (perhaps not where to lay our heads)`, my heart was too full to bear the weight of affliction which I thought just ready to overtake us, and my body too weak almost to bear the shock, unsupported by my better half.

"But, thanks be to Heaven, we are at present relieved from our fears respecting ourselves. I now feel anxious for your safety, but hope prudence will direct to a proper care and attention to yourselves. May this second attempt of Howe's prove his utter ruin. May destruction overtake him as a whirlwind."

John's reply to this letter is characteristic.

"I think I have sometimes observed to you in conversation, that upon examining the biography of illustrious men, you will generally find some female about them, in the relation of mother or wife or sister, to whose instigation a great part of their merit is to be ascribed. You will find a curious example of this in the case of Aspasia, the wife of Pericles. She was a woman of the greatest beauty and the first genius. She taught him, it is said, his refined maxims of policy, his lofty imperial eloquence, nay, even composed the speeches on which so great a share of his reputation was founded. . . .

"I wish some of our great men had such wives.

By the account in your last letter, it seems the women in Boston begin to think themselves able to
serve their country.   What a pity it is that our Generals in the northern districts had not Aspasias to
their wives!

"I believe the two Howes have not very great
women for wives.   If they had, we should suffer
more from their exertions than we do.   This is our
good fortune.   A woman of good sense would not
let her husband spend five weeks at sea in such a
season of the year.   A smart wife would have put
Howe in possession of Philadelphia a long time
ago."

A week later he writes:

"If Howe is gone to Charleston, you will have a
little quiet, and enjoy your corn, and rye, and flax,
and hay and other good things, until another summer.   But what shall we do for sugar and wine and
rum?   Why truly, I believe we must leave them
off.   Loaf sugar is only four dollars a pound here,
and brown only a dollar for the meanest sort, and
ten shillings for that a little better.   Everybody here
is leaving off loaf sugar, and most are laying aside
brown."

Still the prices rose and rose.   On August 29th,
John quotes:

"Prices current. Four pounds a week for board, besides finding your own washing, shaving, candles, liquors, pipes, tobacco, wood, etc. Thirty shillings a week for a servant. It ought to be thirty shillings for a gentleman and four pounds for the servant, because he generally eats twice as much and makes twice as much trouble. Shoes, five dollars a pair. Salt, twenty-seven dollars a bushel. Butter, ten shillings a pound. Punch, twenty shillings a bowl. All the old women and young children are gone down to the Jersey shore to make salt. Salt water is boiling all round the coast, and I hope it will increase. For it is nothing but heedlessness and shiftlessness that prevents us from making salt enough for a supply. But necessity will bring us to it. As to sugar, molasses, rum, etc., we must leave them off. Whiskey is used here instead of rum, and I don't see but it is just as good. Of this the wheat and rye countries can easily distill enough for the use of the country. If I could get cider I would be content."

In September he describes at length the making of molasses out of corn-stalks. "Scarcely a town or parish within forty miles of us but what has several mills at work; and had the experiment been made a month sooner many thousand barrels would have been made. No less than eighty have been made in the small town of Manchester. It answers very well to distill, and may be boiled down to sugar. Thus you see," he adds, "we go from step to step in our improvements. We can live much better than we deserve within ourselves. Why should we borrow foreign luxuries? Why should we wish to bring ruin upon ourselves? I feel as contented when I have breakfasted upon milk as ever I did with Hyson or Souchong. Coffee and sugar I use only as a rarity. There are none of these things but I could totally renounce. My dear friend knows that I could always conform to times and circumstances. As yet I know nothing of hardships. My children have never cried for bread nor been destitute of clothing. Nor have the poor and needy gone empty from my door, whenever it was in my power to assist them."

Though the patriot ladies were ready enough to do without Hyson or Souchong they none the less greatly desired a cheering cup of *something,* and managed to get it without tax or expense. We read of tea made from ribwort, from sage, from thoroughwort, from strawberry and currant leaves. "Hyperion tea," called by a good patriot, "very delicate and most excellent," was made from raspberry leaves; "Liberty tea" from the four-leaved loose-strife. So there was great boiling and steeping going on, and every housewife who had a garden patch, or who was near enough the woods and fields to go out "yarb-gathering," could be sure of a "dish of tay," without thought of King George or his myrmidons.

There was a great harvest, in this year 1777; once more Mother Nature proclaimed herself on the side of Independence. The valleys lay so thick with corn that they did laugh and sing. Most of the able-bodied men being in the field (for the war was now in full swing) there were not enough hands to gather in the crops. Abigail fears that "if it is necessary to make any more drafts upon us, the women must reap the harvests"; and adds, "I am willing to do my part. I believe I could gather corn, and husk it; but I should make a poor figure at digging potatoes."

Indeed, most of the harvesting that autumn was done by women, aided by old men and young boys. Delicate ladies, sturdy farmers' wives and daughters, they worked side by side: and we read that "towards the end of August, at the Forks of Brandywine, girls were harnessing the ploughs, and preparing fallows for the seed, on the very fields where, a twelvemonth from that date, a costly crop of human life was reaped."

The reader of this little book, holding it in his right hand, should hold in his left a history of the United States and should have an atlas "handy by."

Far and wide the war spread : campaign followed campaign : New York, White Plains, Crown Point : our affair is not with them, but with our faithful married lovers, still separated by the long leagues that lie between Massachusetts and Pennsylvania. I must, however, describe briefly what happened in and near Philadelphia, where John Adams and his brother Congressmen were sitting. All through the spring and summer Washington had been harrying the British with varying fortunes. On August 24th, he entered Philadelphia with his army: four regiments of light horse, writes John Adams, four grand divisions of infantry, and the artillery with the matrosses. "They marched twelve deep, and yet took up above two hours in passing by." Washington led the march, and beside him rode the young Marquis de Lafayette, newly arrived ; a lad of nineteen, who had left his young wife and his brilliant circle, to lay his sword at the feet of the American Republic.

This "dress-parade" was not a magnificent one. The soldiers' boots were worn through; their clothes were ragged, and of every hue and style. The least badly dressed among them, we are told, were those who wore the hunting shirt of brown linen. But the brown faces above the shirts were strong and keen, and alight with purpose and resolve; their horses were in prime condition: the green boughs they wore lent a touch of color; there was even a hint of splendor where the Stars and Stripes, newly assembled, fluttered on the breeze. "Fine and war-like troops," Lafayette pronounced them, "commanded by officers of zeal and courage." John Adams writes in sober exultation to Portia:

"The army, upon an accurate inspection of it, I find to be extremely well armed, pretty well clothed, and tolerably disciplined. . . . There is such a mixture of the sublime and the beautiful together with the useful in military discipline, that I wonder every officer we have is not charmed with it." Mr. Adams, after watching the parade, is convinced that he, in military life, should be a decisive disciplinarian. "I am convinced there is no other effective way of indulging benevolence, humanity, and the tender social passions in the army. There is no other way of preserving the health and spirits of the men.

There is no other way of making them active and skilful in war; no other way of guarding an army against destruction by surprises; and no other method of giving them confidence in one another, of making them stand by one another in the hour of battle. Discipline in an army is like the laws of civil society."

Dark days followed. Howe had landed with fresh troops of highly trained soldiers, bent on taking Philadelphia and driving out the Rebel Congress. On September eleventh, Mr. Adams writes:

"The moments are critical here. We know not but the next will bring us an account of a general engagement begun, and when once begun, we know not how it will end, for the battle is not always to the strong. . . . But if it should be the will of Heaven that our army should be defeated, our artillery lost, our best generals killed, and Philadelphia fall in Mr. Howe's hands, still America is not conquered."

Three days later Brandywine was lost and won; then came the fatal night of Paoli, when Anthony Wayne first measured swords with Cornwallis, and found his own the shorter: and on September 26th, the British army entered Philadelphia.

"Don't be anxious about me," John Adams had written on the 14th, "nor about our great and sacred cause. It is the cause of truth and will prevail."

On the 19th, Congress, yielding to the inevitable, removed to Yorktown and there continued its work. Mr. Adams, describing the removal briefly, says, "I shall avoid everything like history, and make no reflections." I hasten to follow his example and return to Braintree.

On October 25th, 1777, Abigail writes:

"The joyful news of the surrender (at Saratoga) of General Burgoyne and all his army, to our victorious troops, prompted me to take a ride this afternoon with my daughter to town, to join, tomorrow, with my friends in thanksgiving and praise to the Supreme Being who hath so remarkably delivered our enemies into our hands. And, hearing that an express is to go off tomorrow morning, I have retired to write you a few lines. I have received no letters from you since you left Philadelphia, by the post, and but one by any private hand. I have written you once before this. Do not fail of writing by the return of this express, and direct your letters to the care of my uncle, who has been a kind and faithful hand to me through the whole season, and a constant attendant upon the post-office."

The leagues were to stretch yet farther between Portia and her dearest friend. A month after this, Mr. Adams asked and obtained leave of Congress to visit his family, mounted his horse, and rode joyfully home to Braintree. We can well imagine the rejoicings that greeted his return; but they were short-lived. He had barely reached home when word came that he was appointed ambassador to France, and that the frigate *Boston* was being prepared to carry him thither as soon as possible.

Here was a thunderbolt indeed! Weary and worn after four years of incessant labor, John Adams had longed almost passionately for the joys and comforts of home life and family affection. He weighed the matter well: the probability of capture on the high seas, of imprisonment or execution in England: the needs of his family, which he had been forced to neglect these four years past. "My children were growing up without my care in their education, and all my emoluments as a member of Congress for four years had not been sufficient to pay a laboring man upon my farm. . . . On the other hand, my country was in deep distress and in great danger. Her dearest interests would be involved in

the relations she might form with foreign nations.
My own plan of these relations had been deliberately
formed and fully communicated to Congress nearly
two years before. The confidence of my country
was committed to me without my solicitation. My
wife, who had always encouraged and animated
me in all antecedent dangers and perplexities, did
not fail me on this occasion. But she discovered an
inclination to bear me company, with all our children. This proposal, however, she was soon convinced, was too hazardous and imprudent."

Help from France was imperative. Franklin was
already there, but greatly needing stronger support.

There was no real question of John Adams' decision: it was soon made, his faithful Portia acqui-
escing without a murmur. She even agreed to
Johnny's going with his father—or proposed it, we
know not which; and preparations were made for
the departure. Fortunately, the frigate took longer
to prepare than the trunks; it was not till February
that all was ready, and the final parting came. Had
it been known that even while he was embarking a
treaty was being signed in Paris between France
and America, this parting might have been delayed.

Mr. Adams' diary gives us glimpses of the voyage, which was a stormy one and threatened other dangers beside. They fell in with some British ships, and one of them gave chase.

"When the night approached, the wind died away, and we were left rolling and pitching in a calm, with our guns all out, our courses drawn up and every way prepared for battle; the officers and men appeared in good spirits and Captain Tucker said his orders were to carry me to France, and to take any prizes that might fall in his way; he thought it his duty, therefore, to avoid fighting, especially with an unequal force, if he could, but if he could not avoid an engagement he would give them something that should make them remember him. I said, and did all in my power, to encourage the officers and men to fight them to the last extremity. My motives were more urgent than theirs; for it will easily be believed that it would have been more eligible for me to be killed on board the *Boston,* or sunk to the bottom in her, than to be taken prisoner. I sat in the cabin, at the windows in the stern, and saw the enemy gaining upon us very fast, she appearing to have a breeze of wind, while we had none. Our powder, cartridges, and balls, were placed by the guns, and everything ready to begin the action. Although it was calm on the surface of the sea, where we lay, the heavens had been gradually overspread with black clouds, and the wind began to spring up. Our ship began to move. The night came on, and it was soon dark. We lost sight of our enemy, who did not appear to me very ardent to overtake us. But the wind increased to a hurricane."

The hurricane proved a terrible one. The diary tells us:

"It would be fruitless to attempt a description of what I saw, heard, and felt, during these three days and nights. To describe the ocean, the waves, the winds; the ship, her motions, rollings, wringings, and agonies; the sailors, their countenances, language, and behavior, is impossible. No man could keep upon his legs and nothing could be kept in its place; an universal wreck of everything in all parts of the ship, chests, casks, bottles, etc. No place or person was dry. On one of these nights, a thunderbolt struck three men upon deck, and wounded one of them a little by a scorch upon his shoulder; it also struck our maintop-mast. . . .

"It is a great satisfaction to me, however, to recollect that I was myself perfectly calm, during the whole. I found, by the opinion of the people aboard, and of the captain himself, that we were in danger, and of this I was certain also, from my own observation: but I thought myself in the way of my duty, and I did not repent of my voyage. I confess I often regretted that I had brought my son. I was not so clear that it was my duty to expose him as myself, but I had been led to it by the child's inclination, and by the advice of all my friends. My Johnny's behavior gave me a satisfaction that I cannot express; fully sensible of our danger, he was constantly endeavoring to bear it with a manly patience, very attentive to me, and his thoughts constantly running in a serious strain."

A few days later came a yet more thrilling event. The log of the *Boston* says:

"Saw a ship to the south-east standing to the westward. Asked the favor of the Hon. John Adams to chase, which was immediately granted. Made sail and gave chase. At 3 p. m. came up with the chase, gave her a gun and she returned me three, one shot of which carried away my mizzen yard. She immediately struck. Out boat. Got the prisoners on board. She proved the ship *Martha* from London, bound to New York. I ordered a prize-master on board, intending to send her to France, but on consulting Mr. Adams, he thought most advisable to send her to America."

Thus Commodore Tucker, comander of the *Boston,* brief and business-like. Mr. Adams notes that "she was a letter of marque, with fourteen guns. She fired upon us, and one of her shot went through our mizzen yard. I happened to be upon the quarter deck, and in the direction from the ship to the yard, so that the ball went directly over my head. We, upon this, turned our broadside, which the instant she saw she struck. Captain Tucker very prudently ordered his officers not to fire."

"I happened to be upon the quarter deck!" Mr. Adams, what were you doing on the quarter deck? You certainly had no business there during a battle. Log and diary are equally discreet, but in his later years Commodore Tucker used to tell the story of that hour; how on discovering the enemy's ship, "neither he nor Mr. Adams could resist the temptation to engage, although against the dictates of prudent duty. Tucker, however, stipulated that Mr. Adams should remain in the lower part of the ship, as a place of safety. But no sooner had the battle commenced, than he was seen on deck, with a musket in his hands, fighting as a common marine. The Commodore peremptorily ordered him below; but called instantly away, it was not until considerable time had elapsed, that he discovered this public minister still at his post, intently engaged in firing upon the enemy. Advancing, he exclaimed, 'Why are you here, sir? I am commanded by the Continental Congress to carry you in safety to Europe, and I will do it;' and, seizing him in his arms, forcibly carried him from the scene of danger."

I trust Master Johnny was safe in his cabin while all this was going on: be very sure that Portia was never told of it, or at least not till long afterward. She, poor lady, was meantime cheering herself as well as she could; visiting the French fleet, just arrived in Boston Harbor, and entertaining some of its officers, who, she thought, were being neglected in Boston town.

"Generals Heath and Hancock have done their part, but very few, if any, private families have any acquaintance with them. Perhaps I feel more anxious to have them distinguished, on account of the near and dear connections I have among them. It would gratify me much, if I had it in my power, to entertain every officer in the fleet."

This letter was written (I think) on a tired or discouraged day, for in it we actually find Portia reproaching her John, a strange thing indeed. His first letter had been all too short for her anxious heart.

"In the very few lines I have received from you, not the least mention is made that you have ever received a line from me. I have not been so parsimonious as my friend,—perhaps I am not so prudent; but I cannot take my pen, with my heart overflowing, and not give utterance to some of the abundance which is in it. Could you, after a thousand fears and anxieties, long expectation, and painful suspense, be satisfied with my telling you that I was well, that I wished you were with me, that my daughter sent her duty, that I had ordered some articles for you, which I hoped would arrive, etc., etc.? By Heaven, if you could, you have changed hearts with some frozen Laplander, or made a voyage to a region that has chilled every drop of your blood; but I will restrain a pen already, I fear, too rash, nor shall it tell you how much I have suffered from this appearance of—inattention."

She adds that the articles sent by Captain Tucker have "arrived safe, and will be of great service to me. Our money is very little better than blank paper. It takes forty dollars to purchase a barrel of cider; fifty pounds lawful for a hundred of sugar, and fifty dollars for a hundred of flour; four dollars per day for a laborer, and find him, which will amount to four more. You will see, by bills drawn before the date of this, that I had taken the method which I was happy in finding you had directed me to. I shall draw for the rest as I find my situation requires. No article that can be named, foreign or domestic, but what costs more than double in hard money what it once sold for."

Poor Portia! poor John! Some of the letters she longed for were taken by the enemy and thrown overboard. John was writing constantly, and Portia's complaining letter was not a consoling one to receive in "Europe, the dullest place in the world," as he calls it. On December 2d, 1778, he writes:

"For Heaven's sake, my dear, don't indulge a thought that it is possible for me to neglect or forget all that is dear to me in this world. It is impossible for me to write as I did in America. What should I write? It is not safe to write anything that one is not willing should go into all the newspapers of the world. I know not by whom to write. I never know what conveyance is safe. . . . I know nothing of many vessels that go from the seaports, and if I knew of all, there are some that I should not trust. Notwithstanding all this, I have written to you not much less than fifty letters. I am astonished that you have received no more. But almost every vessel has been taken. . . . God knows

I don't spend my time in idleness, or in gazing at curiosities. I never wrote more letters, however empty they may have been. But by what I hear, they have been all, or nearly all, taken or sunk. My friends complain that they have not received letters from me. I may as well complain. I have received scarcely any letters from America. I have written three where I have received one."

On Sunday evening, December 27th, Abigail writes a letter that makes our hearts ache with her.

"How lonely are my days! how solitary are my nights! secluded from all society but my two little boys and my domestics. By the mountains of snow which surround me, I could almost fancy myself in Greenland. We have had four of the coldest days I ever knew, and they were followed by the severest snow-storm I ever remember. The wind, blowing like a hurricane for fifteen or twenty hours, rendered it impossible for man or beast to live abroad, and has blocked up the roads so that they are impassable. A week ago I parted with my daughter, at the request of our Plymouth friends, to spend a month with them; so that I am solitary indeed.

"Can the best of friends recollect that for fourteen years past I have not spent a whole winter

alone? Some part of the dismal season has here-
tofore been mitigated and softened by the social
converse and participation of the friend of my
youth.

"How insupportable the idea that three thousand
miles and the vast ocean now divide us! but divide
only our persons, for the heart of my friend is in
the bosom of his partner. More than half a score
of years has so riveted it there, that the fabric which
contains it must crumble into dust ere the particles
can be separated; for

> In one fate, our hearts, our fortunes,
> And our beings blend.

"I cannot describe to you how much I was affected the other day with a Scotch song, which
was sung to me by a young lady in order to divert
a melancholy hour; but it had quite a different effect, and the native simplicity of it had all the
power of a well-wrought tragedy. When I could
conquer my sensibility I begged the song, and Master Charles has learned it, and consoles his mamma
by singing it to her. I will inclose it to you. It
has beauties in it to me which an indifferent person
would not feel, perhaps.

> His very foot has music in 't,
> As he comes up the stairs.

"How oft has my heart danced to the sound of that music!

>And shall I see his face again?
>And shall I hear him speak

"Gracious Heaven! hear and answer my daily petition, by banishing all my grief.

"I am sometimes quite discouraged from writing. So many vessels are taken that there is little chance of a letter's reaching your hands. That I meet with so few returns is a circumstance that lies heavy at my heart. If this finds its way to you, it will go by the *Alliance*. By her I have written before. She has not yet sailed, and I love to amuse myself with my pen, and pour out some of the tender sentiments of a heart overflowing with affection, not for the eye of a cruel enemy, who, no doubt, would ridicule every humane and social sentiment, long ago grown callous to the finer sensibilities, but for the sympathetic heart that beats in unison with

"PORTIA'S."

John replies to this:

"Dr. J. is transcribing your Scotch song, which is a charming one. Oh, my leaping heart!

"I must not write a word to you about politics, because you are a woman.

"What an offense have I committed! A woman!

"I shall soon make it up. I think women better than men, in general, and I know that you can keep a secret as well as any man whatever. But the world don't know this. Therefore if I were to write my sentiments to you, and the letter should be caught and hitched into a newspaper, the world would say I was not to be trusted with a secret."

To us, it need be no secret that there were divisions in the American Legation at Paris. Franklin was at odds with his colleagues, who seem to have been more hindrance than help to him. Moreover, Congress, in the excitement of the treaty, forgot, for a time, all about John Adams and his mission. In short, he came too late for the fair, found no orders, and little to do, save talk with the old philosopher and the Comte de Vergennes. Now and then the diary gives us a sidelight on Franklin.

"Dr. Franklin, upon my saying the other day that I fancied he did not exercise so much as he was wont, answered, 'Yes, I walk a league every day in my chamber; I walk quick, and for an hour, so that I go a league; I make a point of religion of it.' I replied, 'That as the commandment, "thou shalt not kill," forbids a man to kill himself as well as his neighbor, it was manifestly a breach of the sixth commandment not to exercise; so that he might easily prove it to be a religious point.' "

John Adams could not be idle. "I cannot eat pensions and sinecures," he writes: "they would stick in my throat." He was in no mood to follow Franklin's advice and wait quietly for further orders. There was nothing for him to do, and he would go home in the first available ship. Accordingly, on June 17th, 1779, he sailed on the *Sensible,* with son John beside him, and that episode was closed.

All this time the war was going on and prices were rising. Abigail "blushes" while giving John the prices current: "All butcher's meat from a dollar to eight shillings per pound; corn twenty-five dollars, rye thirty, per bushel; flour fifty pounds per hundred; potatoes ten dollars per bushel; butter twelve shillings a pound, cheese eight; sugar twelve shillings a pound; molasses twelve dollars per gallon; labor six and eight dollars a day; a common cow from sixty to seventy pounds; and all English goods in proportion."

By March, labor was eight dollars per day, with twelve dollars in prospect; goods of all kinds at such a price that Abigail hardly dares mention it.

"Linens are sold at twenty dollars per yard; the most ordinary sort of calicoes at thirty and forty; broadcloths at forty pounds per yard; West India goods full as high; molasses at twenty dollars per gallon; sugar four dollars per pound, bohea tea at forty dollars; and our own produce in proportion; butcher's meat at six and eight shillings per pound; board at fifty and sixty dollars per week." She adds:

"In contemplation of my situation, I am sometimes thrown into an agony of distress. Distance, dangers, and oh, I cannot name all the fears which sometimes oppress me, and harrow up my soul. Yet must the common lot of man one day take place, whether we dwell in our own native land or are far distant from it. That we rest under the shadow of the Almighty is the consolation to which I resort, and find that comfort which the world cannot give. If He sees best to give me back my friend, or to preserve my life to him, it will be so."

She little thought that even while she wrote, her friend was spreading his wings—or rather, the broad white wings of the frigate *Sensible,* for his homeward flight.

CHAPTER IX

MR. ADAMS ABROAD

IN AUGUST, 1779, Mr. Adams returned, and all was joy; but again the joy was short-lived. There seemed really no end to the trials of these two loving hearts. In November, Mr. Adams was again ordered to France on public service, and sailed in November. This time he took not only John but little Charles with him, and Abigail's heart was doubly desolate.

"DEAREST OF FRIENDS,—My habitation, how desolate it looks! my table, I sit down to it, but cannot swallow my food! Oh, why was I born with so much sensibility, and why, possessing it, have I so often been called to struggle with it? I wish to see you again. Were I sure you would not be gone, I could not withstand the temptation of coming to town, though my heart would suffer over again the cruel torture of separation.

"What a cordial to my dejected spirits were the few lines last night received! And does your heart forebode that we shall again be happy? My hopes and fears rise alternately. I cannot resign more than I do, unless life itself were called for. My dear sons, I cannot think of them without a tear. Little do they know the feelings of a mother's heart. May they be good and useful as their father! Then they will in some measure reward the anxiety of a mother. My tenderest love to them. Remember me also to Mr. Thaxter, whose civilities and kindness I shall miss.

"God Almighty bless and protect my dearest friend, and, in his own time, restore him to the affectionate bosom of

"PORTIA."

It was all the more lonely for Mrs. Adams that the winter was a severe one: "the sublimest winter" she ever saw. In December and January there fell the highest snow known in forty years; all through January and February, the Bay was frozen over, so that no vessel could pass through for a month. "We had neither snow, rain, nor the least thaw. It has been remarkably healthy, and we have lived along very comfortably, though many people have suffered greatly for food."

In the long winter days, how eagerly Mrs. Adams

must have watched for the incoming mails! I do not know what were the postal arrangements of Braintree; very likely there were none. In Boston, the Post Office was opened every Monday morning from the middle of March to the middle of September, "at 7 of the clock, to deliver out all letters that do come by the post till twelve o'clock; from twelve to two o'clock, being dinner-time, no office kept; and from two o'clock in the afternoon to six o'clock the office will be open to take in all letters to go by the Southern and Western post."

A single letter cost one shilling to send; this rate held to the middle of the nineteenth century. Beside letters, the faithful Portia sent to her John all the papers and news-letters she could lay hands on.

Boston by this time had several newspapers. The first of these, appearing as early as 1704, was the *Boston News-Letter,* "Published by Authority." For some time this little sheet held the field alone; but in 1721 appeared the *Boston Gazette,* and the *New England Courant.* In both these, James Franklin, Benjamin's elder brother, had a hand; indeed, the *Courant* was his own paper, started when he was discharged from the staff of the *Gazette.* He seems to have been a quarrelsome fellow, was twice arraigned for contempt, and once

imprisoned. Benjamin, then a boy of sixteen, as-
tute from his cradle, contributed by stealth to the
Courant more or less; but slipped away to Philadelphia without getting into trouble.

These papers, doubtless, Portia sent regularly to
her John, who received them as often as Fate or
the enemy allowed.

Now and then Mrs. Adams took her chaise and
went into town to make some visits in Boston or
Cambridge.

"Present my compliments to Mr. Dana," she
writes. "Tell him I have called upon his lady, and
we enjoyed an afternoon of sweet communion. I
find she would not be averse to taking a voyage,
should he be continued abroad. She groans most
bitterly, and is irreconcilable to his absence. I am
a mere philosopher to her. I am *inured,* but not
hardened, to the painful portion. Shall I live to
see it otherwise?"

This was written in July, 1780. We may fancy
Madam Abigail setting out on this expedition,
stately and demure in hoop petticoat and high-heeled
shoes. We cannot be sure whether she wore a Leghorn hat or a calash. Here I pause for a moment; I remember a calash, in my childhood. It
was made of thin green silk, shirred on pieces of

rattan or whalebone, placed two or three inches apart. These were drawn together at the back by a cape, and thus, bent into hoop-shape, could be drawn so far over the face as to cover it entirely. The "bashful bonnet," the thing was called; certainly, no headdress ever was uglier, but it must have been "matchless for the complexion," as Madam Patti says of a certain well-known soap.

On the whole, knowing what the calash looked like, I should prefer to think that Madam Abigail wore a Leghorn hat over her fine dark hair. Leghorns were costly. I have heard of their costing twenty-five or even fifty dollars: but they lasted for years and years. It was not till some years after this that American women began to make their own bonnet straw. It became the rage, both here and in England, and women vied with each other in the amount and quality of their "straw-work." Hats and bonnets were not enough; women wore "straw-coats" or *paillasses;* these were made of "sarcenet, calico, or linen, and ornamented profusely with straw." A writer in the *European Magazine* exclaims:

"Straw! straw! everything is ornamented in straw, from the cap to the shoe-buckles; Ceres is the favorite, not only of the female but the male part of the fashionable world, for the gentlemen's waistcoats are ribbed with straw."

Here is a long digression; let us hope that Mrs. Dana gave Mrs. Adams a good dish of tea and that she went home refreshed.

There are but few letters of 1780: probably many were lost. In October Mrs. Adams again quotes the current prices, for which her husband frequently asks.

"You tell me to send you prices current. I will aim at it. Corn is now thirty pounds, rye twenty-seven, per bushel. Flour from a hundred and forty to a hundred and thirty per hundred. Beef, eight dollars per pound; mutton, nine; lamb, six, seven, and eight. Butter, twelve dollars per pound; cheese, ten. Sheep's wool, thirty dollars per pound; flax, twenty. West India articles: sugar, from a hundred and seventy to two hundred pounds per hundred; molasses, forty-eight dollars per gallon; tea, ninety; coffee, twelve; cotton-wool, thirty per pound. Exchange from seventy to seventy-five for hard money. Bills at fifty. Money scarce; plenty of goods; *enormous* taxes."

And what were young John and Charles doing, far from home and mother? They were studying, and improving themselves in every proper way. In

December, 1780, they were sent to Leyden, which Mr. Adams thinks "perhaps as learned a University as any in Europe." He notes in his diary of January, 1781, "John is transcribing a Greek Grammar . . . of his master's composition, and Charles a Latin one; John is also transcribing a treatise on Roman antiquities. . . . After dinner they went to the Rector Magnificus to be matriculated into the University; Charles was found to be too young, none under twelve years of age being admitted; John was admitted after making a declaration that he would do nothing against the laws of the university, city, or land."

I have to exercise stern self-control to keep from quoting too much from Mr. Adams' diary: after all, it is his wife's story that I am trying to tell. Yet—surely never were husband and wife more entirely one—I must indulge myself, and my readers, with his account of the Royal Family of France at supper. He did not admire Queen Marie Antoinette as much as Edmund Burke did, and does not scruple to say so.

"She was an object too sublime and beautiful for my dull pen to describe. I leave this enterprise to Mr. Burke. But, in his description, there is more of the orator than of the philosopher. Her dress was every thing that art and wealth could make it. One of the maids of honor told me she had diamonds upon her person to the value of eighteen millions of livres; and I always thought her majesty much beholden to her dress. Mr. Burke saw her probably but once. I have seen her fifty times perhaps, and in all the varieties of her dresses. She had a fine complexion, indicating perfect health, and was a handsome woman in her face and figure. But I have seen beauties much superior, both in countenance and form, in France, England, and America."

He goes on to describe the spectacle of the *grand couvert*:

"I was selected, and summoned indeed, from all my company, and ordered to a seat close beside the royal family. The seats on both sides of the hall, arranged like the seats in a theatre, were all full of ladies of the first rank and fashion in the kingdom, and there was no room or place for me but in the midst of them. It was not easy to make room, for one more person. However, room was made, and I was situated between two ladies, with rows and ranks of ladies above and below me, and on the right hand and on the left, and ladies only. My dress was a decent French dress, becoming the

JOHN ADAMS
Painted by Gilbert Stuart

station I held, but not to be compared with the gold, and diamonds, and embroidery, about me. I could neither speak, nor understand the language in a manner to support a conversation, but I had soon the satisfaction to find it was a silent meeting, and that nobody spoke a word, but the royal family, to each other, and they said very little. The eyes of all the assembly were turned upon me, and I felt sufficiently humble and mortified, for I was not a proper object for the criticisms of such a company I found myself gazed at, as we in America used to gaze at the sachems who came to make speeches to us in Congress, but I thought it very hard if I could not command as much power of face as one of the chiefs of the Six Nations, and, therefore, determined that I would assume a cheerful countenance, enjoy the scene around me, and observe it as coolly as an astronomer contemplates the stars. . . . The king was the royal carver for himself and all his family. His majesty ate like a king, and made a royal supper of solid beef, and other things in proportion. The queen took a large spoonful of soup, and displayed her fine person and graceful manners, in alternately looking at the company in various parts of the hall, and ordering several kinds of seasoning to be brought to her, by which she fitted her supper to her taste. When this was accomplished, her majesty exhibited to the admiring spectators, the magnificent spectacle of a great queen swallowing her royal supper in a single spoonful all at once. This was all performed like perfect clock work; not a feature of her face, nor a motion of any part of her person, especially her arm and her hand, could be criticized as out of order. A little, and but a little, conversation seemed to pass among the royal personages of both sexes, but in so low a voice, that nothing could be understood by any of the audience.

"The officers about the king's person brought him many letters and papers, from time to time, while he was at table. He looked at these. Some of them he read, or seemed to read, and returned them to the same officers who brought them, or some others.

"These ceremonies and shows may be condemned by philosophy and ridiculed by comedy, with great reason. Yet the common sense of mankind has never adopted the rigid decrees of the former, nor ever sincerely laughed with the latter. Nor has the religion of nations, in any age, approved of the dogmas or the satires. On the contrary, it has always overborne them all, and carried its inventions of such exhibitions to a degree of sublimity and pathos, which has frequently transported the greatest infidels out of themselves. Something of the kind every government and every religion has, and must have; and the business and duty of law-givers and philosophers is to endeavor to prevent them from being carried too far."

Mr. Adams is full of anxieties:

"I am sorry to learn you have a sum of paper. How could you be so imprudent? You must be frugal, I assure you. Your children will be poorly off. I can but barely live in the manner that is indispensably demanded of me by everybody. Living is dear indeed here. My children will not be so well left by their father as he was by his. They will be infected with the examples and habits and tastes for expensive living without the means. He was not. My children shall never have the smallest soil of dishonor or disgrace brought upon them by their father, no, not to please ministers, kings, or nations. At the expense of a little of this, my children might perhaps ride at their ease through life, but dearly as I love them, they shall live in the service of their country, in her navy, her army, or even out of either in the extremest degree of poverty, before I will depart in the smallest iota from my sentiments of honor and delicacy; for I, even I, have sentiments of delicacy as exquisite as the proudest minister that ever served a monarch. They may not be exactly like those of some ministers. . . .

"General Washington has done me great honor and much public service by sending me authentic accounts of his own and General Greene's last great actions. They are in the way to negotiate peace. It lies wholly with them. No other ministers but they and their colleagues in the army can accomplish the great event.

"I am keeping house, but I want a housekeeper. What a fine affair it would be, if we could flit across the Atlantic as they say the angels do from planet to planet! I would dart to Penn's Hill and bring you over on my wings; but, alas, we must keep house separately for some time. But one thing I am determined on. If God should please to restore me once more to your fireside, I will never again leave it without your ladyship's company— no, not even to go to Congress to Philadelphia, and there I am determined to go, if I can make interest enough to get chosen, whenever I return. I would give a million sterling that you were here; and I could afford it as well as Great Britain can the thirty millions she must spend, the ensuing year, to complete her own ruin. Farewell, farewell."

I like to picture John Adams as he wrote those words: sitting erect at his desk, his chin up, his eyes flashing. So, I fancy, he may have looked, in his "decent French dress" in the crowd of court ladies, that evening at Versailles.

More and more as time went on, did the two friends long for each other. I say "friends," because it is their own word; most of the letters begin with it. Abigail writes:

"MY DEAREST FRIEND,—The family are all retired to rest; the busy scenes of the day are over; a day which I wished to have devoted in a particular manner to my dearest friend; but company falling in prevented it, nor could I claim a moment until this silent watch of the night.

"Look (is there a dearer name than *friend?* Think of it for me), look to the date of this letter, and tell me what are the thoughts which arise in your mind. Do you not recollect that eighteen years have run their circuit since we pledged our mutual faith to each other, and the hymeneal torch was lighted at the altar of Love? Yet, yet it burns with unabating fervor. Old Ocean has not quenched it, nor old Time smothered it in this bosom. It cheers me in the lonely hour; it comforts me even in the gloom which sometimes possesses my mind."

She begs to be allowed to join him in Europe.

"I have repeatedly expressed my desire to make a part of your family. But 'Will you come and see me?' cannot be taken in that serious light I should choose to consider an invitation from those I love. I do not doubt but that you would be glad to see me, but I know you are apprehensive of dangers and fatigues. I know your situation may be unsettled, and it may be more permanent than I wish it. Only think how the words, 'three, four, and five years' absence,' sound! They sink into my heart with a weight I cannot express. Do you look like the miniature you sent? I cannot think so. But you have a better likeness, I am told. Is that designed for me? Gracious Heavens! restore to me the original, and I care not who has the shadow."

John was fully convinced that Portia would not like Paris, and that it would not agree with her or the children. "It would be most for the happiness of my family," he says, "and most for the honor of our country, that I should come home. I have, therefore, this day written to Congress a resignation of all my employments, and as soon as I shall receive their acceptance of it, I will embark for America, which will be in the spring or beginning of summer. Our son is now on his journey from Petersburg, through Sweden, Denmark, and Germany, and if it please God he come safe, he shall come with me, and I pray we may all meet once more, you and I never to separate again."

It was about this time that "a person" asked Mrs. Adams, "If you had known that Mr. Adams should have remained so long abroad, would you have consented that he should have gone?"

"I recollected myself a moment," says Portia, "and then spoke the real dictates of my heart: 'If I had known, sir, that Mr. Adams could have effected what he has done, I would not only have submitted to the absence I have endured, painful as it has been, but I would not have opposed it, even though three years more should be added to the number (which Heaven avert!). I feel a pleasure in being able to sacrifice my selfish passions to the general good, and in imitating the example which has taught me to consider myself and family but as the small dust of the balance, when compared with the great community.'"

And now the long separation was to end. In December, 1782, Mr. Adams writes:

"Whether there should be peace or war, I shall come home in the summer. As soon as I shall receive from Congress their acceptance of the resignation of all my employments, which I have transmitted many ways, I shall embark, and you may depend upon a good domestic husband for the remainder of my life, if it is the will of Heaven that I should once more meet you. My promises are not lightly made with anybody. I have never broken one made to you, and I will not begin at this time of life.

"My children, I hope, will once at length discover that they have a father who is not unmindful of their welfare. They have had too much reason to think themselves forgotten, although I know that an anxiety for their happiness has corroded me every day of my life.

"With a tenderness which words cannot express, I am theirs and yours forever."

The war was over; the child Independence had grown to full stature, and the Republic took her place among the nations. On the 21st of January, 1783, articles of peace were drawn up between Great Britain, France, and the United States.

CHAPTER X

THE COURT OF ST. JAMES

NOT yet, Abigail! The treaty of peace was signed on the 21st of January, 1783; but Congress refused to John Adams the leisure he had so amply earned, and so ardently desired. A treaty of commerce must be established between Great Britain and the United States, and he, with Benjamin Franklin and John Jay, must make it. The faithful patriot accepted the new charge without hesitation, but this time his body rebelled. He fell dangerously ill of a fever, brought on by anxiety and over-work. For some days his life hung in the balance: but he could not die then. His work was not done. Barely recovered, while still weak and suffering, he hastened to London, to take up the new task. This accomplished, another waited him. Orders came for him to go at once to Holland, to obtain a loan for the new Republic. This, he felt, might well be the last straw for him; yet he did not falter.

"It was winter. My health was very delicate. A journey and voyage to Holland at that season would very probably put an end to my labors. I scarcely saw a possibility of surviving it. Nevertheless, no man knows what he can bear till he tries. A few moment's reflection determined me; for although I had little hope of getting the money, having experienced so many difficulties before, yet making the attempt and doing all in my power would discharge my own conscience, and ought to satisfy my responsibility to the public."

Here follows a detailed account of the trip, which I exercise much self-control not to quote. He adds:

"I had ridden on horseback often to Congress, over roads and across ferries, of which the present generation have no idea; and once, in 1777, in the dead of winter, from Braintree to Baltimore, five hundred miles, upon a trotting horse, as Dean Swift boasted that he had done or could do. I had been three days in the Gulf Stream, in 1778, in a furious hurricane and a storm of thunder and lightning, which struck down our men upon deck, and cracked our mainmast; when the oldest officers and stoutest seamen stood aghast, at their last prayers, dreading every moment that a butt would start, and all perish. I had crossed the Atlantic, in 1779, in a leaky ship, with perhaps four hundred men on board, who were scarcely able, with two large pumps going all the twenty-four hours, to keep water from filling the hold, in hourly danger, for twenty days together, of foundering at sea. I had passed the mountains in Spain, in the winter, among ice and snow, partly on mule-back and partly on foot; yet I never suffered so much in any of these situations as in that jaunt from Bath to Amsterdam, in January, 1784. Nor did any of those adventures ever do such lasting injuries to my health. I never got over it till my return home, in 1788."

Still the tasks multiplied; still the Hills of Difficulty rose before the devoted statesman. Finally, in the summer of 1784, seeing his return home indefinitely postponed, he dismissed his anxieties and summoned his faithful Portia to his side. She sailed on the 20th of June, on the ship *Active*.

It was her first voyage, and she did not enjoy it. There are no more letters to her "dearest friend"; the faithful pair were not to be separated again for any length of time; but she writes a little every day to her sister, Mrs. Cranch, and does full justice to the discomforts of life in a small sailing vessel.

"Of this I am very sure, that no lady would ever

wish a second time to try the sea, were the objects of her pursuit within the reach of a land journey. I have had frequent occasion, since I came on board, to recollect an observation of my best friend's, 'that no being in nature was so disagreeable as a lady at sea,' and this recollection has in a great measure reconciled me to the thought of being at sea without him; for one would not wish, my dear sister, to be thought of in that light by those, to whom we would wish to appear in our best array. The decency and decorum of the most delicate female must in some measure yield to the necessities of nature; and, if you have no female capable of rendering you the least assistance, you will feel grateful to any one who will feel for you, and relieve or compassionate your sufferings."

She was woefully seasick at first, poor lady. After a time she felt better and writes: "The ship has gradually become less irksome to me. If our cook was but tolerably clean, I could relish my food. But he is a great, dirty, lazy negro, with no more knowledge of cookery than a savage, nor any kind of order in the distribution of his dishes; but on they come, higgledy-piggledy, with a leg of pork all bristly; a quarter of an hour after, a pudding, or perhaps, a pair of roast fowls, first of all, and then will follow one by one a piece of beef, and when dinner is nearly completed, a plate of potatoes. Such a fellow is a real imposition upon the passengers. But gentlemen know but little about the matter, and if they can get enough to eat five times a day, all goes well. We ladies have not eaten, upon our whole passage, more than just enough to satisfy nature, or to keep body and soul together."

Her first impression of England was more exciting than agreeable. Driving to London in a post chaise, "from Chatham we proceeded on our way as fast as possible, wishing to pass Blackheath before dark. Upon this road, a gentleman alone in a chaise passed us, and very soon a coach before us stopped, and there was a hue and cry, 'A robbery, a robbery!' The man in the chaise was the person robbed, and this in open day with carriages constantly passing. We were not a little alarmed, and everyone was concealing his money. Every place we passed and every post chaise we met was crying out, 'A robbery!' Where the thing is so common, I was surprised to see such an alarm. The robber was pursued and taken in about two miles, and we saw the poor wretch, ghastly and horrible, brought along on foot: his horse ridden by a person who took him, who also had his pistol. He looked like a youth of twenty only, attempting to lift his hat, and looked despair. You can form some idea of my feelings when they told him, 'Ay, you have but a short time; the assize sits next month; and then, my lad, you swing.' Though every robber may deserve death, yet to exult over the wretched is what *our* country is not accustomed to. Long may it be free from such villanies, and long may it preserve a commiseration for the wretched."

At last she found herself in London, at Osborne's new family hotel, "Adelphi," where rooms had been engaged for her. Mr. Adams was at the Hague, detained by public business; Portia must be patient as she might.

"Here we have," she writes, "a handsome drawing-room, genteelly furnished, and a large lodging-room. We are furnished with a cook, chambermaid, waiter, etc., for three guineas a week; but in this is not included a mouthful of victuals or drink, all of which is to be paid for separately."

There was now little leisure for writing, for callers came thick and fast. Mr. This, Mrs. That, Dr. the Other, all thronged to pay their respects. Many of these were former friends and neighbors of the Tory persuasion, living in more or less willing exile. "I hardly know how to think myself out of my

own country, I see so many Americans about me."
She knows that her sister will desire news of the
fashions.

"I am not a little surprised to find dress, unless
upon public occasion, so little regarded here. The
gentlemen are very plainly dressed, and the ladies
much less so than with us. 'Tis true, you must put
a hoop on and have your hair dressed, but a common straw hat, no cap, with only a ribbon upon the
crown, is thought sufficient to go into company.
Muslins are much in taste; no silks but lutestrings
worn; but send not to London for any article you
want; you may purchase any thing you can name
much lower in Boston. . . . Our country, alas! our
country! they are extravagant to astonishment in
entertainments compared with what Mr. Smith and
Mr. Storer tell me of this. You will not find at a
gentleman's table more than two dishes of meat,
though invited several days beforehand. . . . At
my lodgings I am as quiet as at any place in Boston; nor do I feel as if it could be any other place
than Boston; Dr. Clark visits us every day; says
he cannot feel at home anywhere else; declares he
has not seen a handsome woman since he came into
the city; that every old woman looks like Mrs.
H——, and every young one like—like the D—l.

They paint here nearly as much as in France, but with more art. The head-dress disfigures them in the eye of an American. I have seen many ladies, but not one elegant one since I came; there is not to me that neatness in their appearance, which you see in our ladies.

"The American ladies are much admired here by the gentlemen, I am told, and in truth I wonder not at it. O, my country, my country! preserve, preserve the little purity and simplicity of manners you yet possess. Believe me, they are jewels of inestimable value; the softness, peculiarly characteristic of our sex, and which is so pleasing to the gentlemen, is wholly laid aside here for the masculine attire and manners of Amazonians."

A few days later, she describes one of the numerous dinners to which she was invited.

"After we had dined, which was in company with five American gentlemen, we retired to the drawing room, and there I talked off the lady's reserve, and she appeared agreeable. Her dress pleased me, and answered to the universal neatness of the apartments, furniture, and entertainment. It was a delicate blue and white copper-plate calico, with a blue lutestring skirt, flounced; a muslin apron and handkerchief, which are much more worn than gauze;

her hair, a fine black, dressed without powder, with a fashionable cap, and straw ribbons upon her head and breast, with a green morocco slipper. Our dinner consisted of fried fish of a small kind, a boiled ham, a fillet of veal, a pair of roast ducks, an almond pudding, currants and gooseberries, which in this country are very fine. Painted muslin is much worn here; a straw hat with a deep crown, lined, and a white, green, or any colored ribbon you choose."

The visitors came and went, and Mrs. Adams received them graciously, and returned their visits, and wrote to sisters and nieces; but all the time her heart was in Holland, and she found the days long and weary that kept her friend from her. At last, —at long, long last—the Great Day came. On August 7th, Mr. Adams writes in his diary:

"Arrived at the Adelphi Buildings (London) and met my wife and daughter, after a separation of four years and a half; indeed, after a separation of ten years, excepting a few visits. Set off the next day for Paris."

September, 1784, found the Adamses settled at Auteuil, four miles from Paris, in much contentment, after the long years of separation. Mrs. Adams writes to her sister, Mrs. Cranch:

"The house is much larger than we have need

of : upon occasion, forty beds may be made in it.
I fancy it must be very cold in winter.   There are
few houses with the privilege which this enjoys,
that of having the saloon, as it is called, the apartment where we receive company, upon the first
floor. This room is very elegant, and about a third
larger than General Warren's hall. . . . But with
an expense of thirty thousand livres in looking-
glasses there is no table in the house better than
an oak board, nor a carpet belonging to the house.
The floors I abhor, made of red tiles in the shape
of Mrs. Quincy's floor-cloth tiles. These floors will
by no means bear water, so that the method of clean-
ing them is to have them waxed, and then a manservant with foot brushes drives round your room
dancing here and there like a Merry Andrew. This
is calculated to take from your foot every atom of
dirt, and leave the room in a few moments as he
found it. The dining-rooms, of which you make no
other use, are laid with small stones, like the red
tiles for shape and size. The servants' apartments
are generally upon the first floor, and the stairs
which you commonly have to ascend to get into the
family apartments are so dirty, that I have been
obliged to hold up my clothes, as though I was
passing through a cow-yard."

She finds living in Paris very expensive; more-over, some of the expenses seem to her republican mind unreasonable. "There is now a Court mourn-ing, and every foreign minister, with his family, must go into mourning for a Prince of eight years old, whose father is an ally to the King of France. This mourning is ordered by the Court, and is to be worn for eleven days only. Poor Mr. Jefferson had to hie away for a tailor to get a whole black silk suit made up in two days; and at the end of eleven days, should another death happen, he will be obliged to have a new suit of mourning, of cloth, because that is the season when silk must be left off. We may groan and scold, but these are ex-penses which cannot be avoided; for fashion is the deity everyone worships in this country, and, from the highest to the lowest, you must submit."

In a letter to her niece, Betsey Cranch, she de-scribes the house in greater detail, and dwells with delight on the beauty of the garden. "But Paris, you must not ask me how I like it, because I am going to tell you of the pretty little apartment next to this in which I am writing. Why, my dear, you cannot turn yourself in it without being multiplied twenty times; now that I do not like, for being rather clumsy, and by no means an elegant figure,

I hate to have it so often repeated to me. This room is about ten or twelve feet large, is eight-cornered and panelled with looking-glasses; a red and white India patch, with pretty borders encompasses it; low back stuffed chairs with garlands of flowers encircling them, adorn this little chamber; festoons of flowers are round all the glasses; a lustre hangs from the ceiling adorned with flowers; a beautiful sofa is placed in a kind of alcove, with pillows and cushions in abundance, the use of which I have not yet investigated; in the top of this alcove, over the sofa in the ceiling is another glass; here is a beautiful chimney piece, with an elegant painting of rural life in a country farm-house, lads and lasses jovial and happy. This little apartment opens into your cousin's bed-chamber; it has a most pleasing view of the garden, and it is that view which always brings my dear Betsey to my mind, and makes me long for her to enjoy the delights of it with me."

Mrs. Adams certainly did not like Paris. "They tell me I am no judge, for that I have not seen it yet. One thing I know, and that is that I have smelt it. . . . It is the very dirtiest place I ever saw. . . . Boston cannot boast so elegant public buildings; but, in every other respect, it is as much superior in my eyes to Paris, as London is to Boston."

It is hard to choose among these sprightly letters, so full of color and gayety. Here is an account of the Marquise de Lafayette, written to Mrs. Cranch:

"The Marquise met me at the door, and with the freedom of an old acquaintance, and the rapture peculiar to the ladies of this nation, caught me by the hand and gave me a salute upon each cheek, most heartily rejoiced to see me. You would have supposed I had been some long absent friend, whom she dearly loved. She presented me to her mother and sister, who were present with her, all sitting together in her bed-room, quite *en famille*. One of the ladies was knitting. The Marquise herself was in a chintz gown. She is a middle-sized lady, sprightly and agreeable; and professes herself strongly attached to Americans. She supports an amiable character, is fond of her children, and very attentive to them, which is not the general character of ladies of high rank in Europe. In a few days, she returned my visit, upon which we sent her a card of invitation to dine. She came; we had a large company. There is not a lady in our country, who would have gone abroad to dine so little dressed; and one of our fine American ladies, who sat by me, whispered to me, 'Good Heavens! how awfully she is dressed.' I could not forbear returning the whisper, which I most sincerely despised, by replying that the lady's rank sets her above the little formalities of dress. She had on a Brown Florence gown and petticoat,—which is the only silk, excepting satins, which are worn here in winter—a plain double gauze handkerchief, a pretty cap with a white ribbon in it, and looked very neat. The rouge, 'tis true, was not so artfully laid on, as upon the faces of the American ladies who were present. Whilst they were glittering with diamonds, watch-chains, girdle-buckles, etc., the Marquise was nowise ruffled by her own different appearance. A really well-bred French lady has the most ease in her manners, that you can possibly conceive of. It is studied by them as an art, and they render it nature. It requires some time, you know, before any fashion quite new becomes familiar to us. The dress of the French ladies has the most taste and variety in it, of any I have yet seen; but these are topics I must reserve to amuse my young acquaintance with. I have seen none, however, who carry the extravagance of dress to such a height as the Americans who are here, some of whom, I have reason to think, live at an expense double what is allowed to the American ministers.

They must however, abide the consequences."

The months spent in France proved interesting enough When in May, 1785, Mr. Adams was appointed United States Minister Plenipotentiary to Great Britain, his wife had some things to regret, though more to anticipate. "Delightful and blooming garden, how much I shall regret your loss! . . . It will not be easy to find in the midst of a city so charming a scene."

But Paris was soon forgotten in the excitement of the London season. London was very full this May and June. The Adamses had hard work to find a house, but were finally established in lodgings "at the moderate price of a guinea per day, for two rooms and two chambers at the Bath Hotel, Westminster, Piccadilly."

The first great event was the presentation to Royalty, first of Mr. Adams in private, then of the family, in public. Mrs. Adams notes rather ruefully that "one is obliged here to attend the circles of the Queen, which are held in summer once a fortnight, but once a week the rest of the year; and what renders it exceedingly expensive is, that you cannot go twice the same season in the same dress, and a Court dress you cannot make use of anywhere else." This was hard indeed for people of moderate means and simple tastes; but as usual, Mrs. Adams was mistress of the emergency.

"I directed my mantuamaker to let my dress be elegant, but plain as I could possibly appear, with decency; accordingly, it is white lutestring, covered and full trimmed with white crape, festooned with lilac ribbon and mock point lace, over a hoop of enormous extent; there is only a narrow train of about three yards in length to the gown waist, which is put into a ribbon upon the left side, the Queen only having her train borne. Ruffle cuffs for married ladies, treble lace ruffles, a very dress cap with long lace lappets, two white plumes, and a blonde lace handkerchief. This is my rigging. I should have mentioned two pearl pins in my hair, ear-rings and necklace of the same kind."

On the day of the festivities she writes: "My head is dressed for St. James's, and in my opinion, looks very tasty. Whilst my daughter's is undergoing the same operation, I set myself down composedly to write you a few lines. 'Well,' methinks I hear Betsey and Lucy say, 'what is cousin's dress?' White, my dear girls, like your aunt's, only differently trimmed and ornamented; her train being wholly of white crape, and trimmed with white ribbon; the petticoat, which is the most showy part of the dress, covered and drawn up in what are called festoons, with light wreaths of beautiful flowers; the sleeves white crape, drawn over the silk, with a row of lace round the sleeve near the shoulder, another half way down the arm, and a third upon the top of the ruffle, a little flower stuck between; a kind of hat-cap, with three large feathers and a bunch of flowers; a wreath of flowers upon the hair. Thus equipped, we go in our own carriage, and Mr. Adams and Colonel Smith in his. But I must quit my pen to put myself in order for the ceremony, which begins at two o'clock. When I return, I will relate to you my reception; but do not let it circulate, as there may be persons eager to catch at every thing, and as much given to misrepresentation as here. I would gladly be excused the ceremony."

The next day she thus continues: "Congratulate me, my dear sister, it is over. I was too much fatigued to write a line last evening. At two o'clock we went to the circle, which is in the drawing-room of the Queen. We passed through several apartments, lined as usual with spectators upon these occasions. . . . We were placed in a circle round the drawing-room, which was very full. I believe two hundred persons present. Only think of the task! The royal family have to go round to every person, and find small talk enough to speak to all of them, though they very prudently speak in a whisper, so that only the person who stands next you can hear what is said. The King enters the room, and goes round to the right; the Queen and Princesses to the left. The lord-in-waiting presents you to the King; and the lady-in-waiting does the same to her Majesty. The King is a personable man, but, my dear sister, he has a certain countenance, which you and I have often remarked; a red face and white eyebrows. The Queen has a similar countenance, and the numerous royal family confirm the observation. Persons are not placed according to their rank in the drawing-room, but promiscuously; and when the King comes in, he takes persons as they stand. When he came to me, Lord Onslow said, 'Mrs. Adams'; upon which I drew off my right-hand glove, and his Majesty saluted my left cheek; then asked me if I had taken a walk today. I could have told his Majesty that I had been all the morning preparing to wait upon him; but I replied, 'No, Sire.' 'Why, don't you love walking?' says he. I answered, that I was rather indolent in that respect. He then bowed and passed on. It was more than two hours after this

before it came to my turn to be presented to the
Queen. The circle was so large that the company
were four hours standing. The Queen was evi-
dently embarrassed when I was presented to her. I
had disagreeable feelings, too. She, however, said,
'Mrs. Adams, have you got into your house? Pray,
how do you like the situation of it?' Whilst the
Princess Royal looked compassionate, and asked me
if I was not much fatigued; and observed, that it
was a very full drawing-room. Her sister, who
came next, Princess Augusta, after having asked
your niece if she was ever in England before, and
her answering, 'Yes,' inquired of me how long ago,
and supposed it was when she was very young.
And all this is said with much affability, and the
ease and freedom of old acquaintance. The manner in which they make their tour round the room
is, first, the Queen, the lady-in-waiting behind her,
holding up her train; next to her, the Princess
Royal; after her, Princess Augusta, and their lady-
in-waiting behind them. They are pretty, rather
than beautiful, well shaped, with fair complexions,
and a tincture of the King's countenance. The two
sisters look much alike; they were both dressed in
black and silver silk, with a silver netting upon the
coat, and their heads full of diamond pins. The

Queen was in purple and silver. She is not well shaped nor handsome. As to the ladies of the Court, rank and title may compensate for want of personal charms; but they are, in general, very plain, ill-shaped, and ugly; but don't tell anybody that I say so."

Mrs. Adams did not enjoy Court occasions. "I know," she says to Sister Mary, "I am looked down upon with a sovereign pride, and the smile of royalty is bestowed as a mighty boon. As such, however, I cannot receive it. I know it is due to my country, and I consider myself as complimenting the power before which I appear as much as I am complimented by being noticed by it. With these ideas, you may be sure my countenance will never wear that suppliant appearance, which begs for notice. Consequently I never expect to be a Court favorite. Nor would I ever again set my foot there, if the etiquette of my country did not require it. But, whilst I am in a public character, I must submit to the penalty; for such I shall ever esteem it."

In the same letter she describes one of the Queen's 'drawing-rooms.'

"The company were very brilliant, and her Majesty was stiff with diamonds; the three eldest Princesses and the Prince of Wales were present.

His Highness looked much better than when I saw him before. He is a stout, well-made man, and would look very well if he had not sacrificed so much to Bacchus. The Princess Elizabeth I never saw before. She is about fifteen; a short, clumsy miss, and would not be thought handsome if she was not a princess. The whole family have one complexion, and all are inclined to be corpulent. I should know them in any part of the world. Notwithstanding the English boast so much of their beauties, I do not think they have really so much of it as you will find amongst the same proportion of people in America."

Mrs. Siddons was then in her glory, and Abigail did not fail to see her, and to describe her to the sisterhood at home. This time it is Sister Shaw who hears how "the first piece I saw her in was Shakespeare's 'Othello.' She was interesting beyond any actress I had ever seen; but I lost much of the pleasure of the play, from the sooty appearance of the Moor. Perhaps it may be early prejudice; but I could not separate the African color from the man, nor prevent that disgust and horror which filled my mind every time I saw him touch the gentle Desdemona; nor did I wonder that Brabantio thought some love potion or some witch-

craft had been practised to make his daughter fall
in love with what she scarcely dared look upon.

"I have been more pleased with her since, in several other characters, particularly in Matilda in
'The Carmelite,' a play which I send you for your
amusement. Much of Shakespeare's language is so
uncouth that it sounds very harsh. He has beauties which are not equalled; but I should suppose
they might be rendered much more agreeable for
the stage by alterations. I saw Mrs. Siddons a few
evenings ago in 'Macbeth,' a play, you recollect,
full of horror. She supported her part with great
propriety; but she is too great to be put in so de-
testable a character. . . . You must make as much
interest here to get a box when she plays, as to get
a place at Court; and they are usually obtained in
the same way. It would be very difficult to find the
thing in this country which money will not purchase,
provided you can bribe high enough.

"What adds much to the merit of Mrs. Siddons,
is her virtuous character; slander itself never having slurred it. She is married to a man who bears
a good character; but his name and importance
are wholly swallowed up in her fame. She is the
mother of five children; but from her looks you
would not imagine her more than twenty-five years

old. She is happy in having a brother who is one of the best tragic actors upon the stage, and always plays the capital parts with her; so that both her husband and the virtuous part of the audience can see them in the tenderest scenes without once fearing for their reputation."

To Thomas Jefferson she wrote on June 6, 1785: "I went last week to hear the music (Handel's) in Westminster. 'The Messiah' was performed. It was sublime beyond description. I most sincerely wished for your presence, as your favorite passion would have received the highest gratification. I should have sometimes fancied myself amongst a higher order of Beings if it had not been for a very troublesome female, who was unfortunately seated behind me; and whose volubility not all the powers of music could still."

Mrs. Adams was certainly an admirable correspondent; the long years of separation from her "dearest friend" had taught her how letters were longed for by those at home; and she writes without stint to sisters, nieces and friends. Here are two letters to Betsey and Lucy Cranch, describing the gayeties of London:

"I believe I once promised to give you an ac-

count of that kind of visiting called a ladies' rout.
There are two kinds; one where a lady sets apart
a particular day in the week to see company. These
are held only five months in the year, it being quite
out of fashion to be seen in London during the
summer. When a lady returns from the country
she goes round and leaves a card with all her acquaintances, and then sends them an invitation to
attend her routs during the season. The other kind
is where a lady sends to you for certain evenings,
and the cards are always addressed in her own
name, both to gentlemen and ladies. The rooms
are all set open, and card-tables set in each room,
the lady of the house receiving her company at the
door of the drawing-room, where a set number of
courtesies are given and received with as much order as is necessary for a soldier who goes through
the different evolutions of his exercise. The visitor
then proceeds into the room without appearing to
notice any other person, and takes her seat at the
card table.

> Nor can the muse her aid impart,
> Unskilled in all the terms of art,
> Nor in harmonious numbers put
> The deal, the shuffle, and the cut;
> Go, Tom, and light the ladies up,
> It must be one before we sup.

"At these parties it is usual for each lady to play a rubber, as it is termed, when you must lose or win a few guineas. To give each a fair chance, the lady then rises and gives her seat to another set. It is no unusual thing to have your rooms so crowded that not more than half the company can sit at once, yet this is called *society and polite life*. They treat their company with coffee, tea, lemonade, orgeat and cake. I know of but one agreeable circumstance attending these parties, which is, that you may go away when you please without disturbing anybody. I was early in the winter invited to Madame de Pinto's, the Portuguese minister's. I went accordingly. There were about two hundred persons present. I knew not a single lady but by sight, having met them at Court; and it is an established rule, that though you were to meet as often as three nights in the week, never to speak together, or know each other, unless particularly introduced. I was, however, at no loss for conversation, Madame de Pinto being very polite, and the Foreign Ministers being the most of them present, who had dined with us, and to whom I had been early introduced. It being *Sunday* evening, I declined playing cards; indeed, I always get excused when I can. And Heavens forbid I should catch the manner living as they rise.

". . . At eight o'clock we returned home in order
to dress ourselves for the ball at the French ambassador's, to which we had received an invitation a fortnight before. He has been absent ever
since our arrival here, till three weeks ago. He
has a levee every Sunday evening, at which there
are usually several hundred persons. The Hotel
de France is beautifully situated, fronting St.
James's Park, one end of the house standing upon
Hyde Park. It is a most superb building. About
half past nine, we went and found some company
collected. Many very brilliant ladies of the first
distinction were present. The dancing commenced
about ten, and the rooms soon filled. The room
which he had built for this purpose is large enough
for five or six hundred persons. It is most ele-
gantly decorated, hung with a gold tissue, ornamented with twelve brilliant cut lustres, each con-
tained twenty-four candles. At one end there are
two large arches; these were adorned with wreaths
and bunches of artificial flowers upon the walls; in
the alcoves were cornucopiae, loaded with oranges,
sweetmeats, etc. Coffee, tea, lemonade, orgeat, etc.,
were taken here by every person who chose to go

for them. There were covered seats all round the
room for those who did not choose to dance. In
the other rooms, card-tables, and a large faro-table,
were set: this is a new kind of game, which is much
practised here. Many of the company who did not
dance, retired here to amuse themselves. . . ."

This was Betsey's letter: Lucy was to hear about
the dresses:

"To amuse you then, my dear niece, I will give
you an account of the dress of the ladies at the
ball of the Comte d'Adhémar; as your cousin tells
me that she some time ago gave you a history of
the birthday and ball at Court, this may serve as
a counterpart. Though, should I attempt to compare the apartments, St. James's would fall as much
short of the French Ambassador's as the Court of
his Britannic Majesty does of the splendor and mag-
nificence of that of his Most Christian Majesty.
I am sure I never saw an assembly room in America,
which did not exceed that at St. James's in point
of elegance and decoration; and, as to its fair visitors, not all their blaze of diamonds, set off with
Parisian rouge, can match the blooming health, the
sparkling eye, and modest deportment of the dear
girls of my native land. As to the dancing, the
space they had to move in gave them no opportunity

to display the grace of a minuet, and the full dress of long court-trains and enormous hoops, you well know were not favorable for country dances, so that I saw them at every disadvantage; not so the other evening. They were much more properly clad :—silk waists, gauze or white or painted tiffany coats decorated with ribbon, beads, or flowers, as fancy directed, were chiefly worn by the young ladies. Hats turned up at the sides with diamond loops and buttons of steel, large bows of ribbons and wreaths of flowers, displayed themselves to much advantage upon the heads of some of the prettiest girls England can boast. The light from the lustres is more favorable to beauty than daylight, and the color acquired by dancing, more becoming than rouge, as fancy dresses are more favorable to youth than the formality of a uniform. There was as great a variety of pretty dresses, borrowed wholly from France, as I have ever seen; and amongst the rest, some with sapphire-blue satin waists, spangled with silver, and laced down the back and seams with silver stripes; white satin petticoats trimmed with black and blue velvet ribbon; an odd kind of head-dress, which they term the 'helmet of Minerva.' I did not observe the bird of wisdom, however, nor do I know whether those

who wore the dress had suitable pretensions to it.
'And pray,' say you, 'how were my aunt and cousin
dressed?' If it will gratify you to know, you shall
hear. Your aunt then wore a full-dress court cap
without the lappets, in which was a wreath of white
flowers, and blue sheafs, two black and blue flat
feathers (which cost her half a guinea a-piece, but
that you need not tell of), three pearl pins, bought
for Court, and a pair of pearl ear-rings, the cost of
them—no matter what; no less than diamonds,
however. A sapphire blue *demi-saison* with a satin
stripe, sack and petticoat trimmed with a broad
black lace; crape flounce, etc.; leaves made of blue
ribbon, and trimmed with white floss; wreaths of
black velvet ribbon spotted with steel beads, which
are much in fashion, and brought to such perfection
as to resemble diamonds; white ribbon also in the
Vandyke style, made up the trimming, which
looked very elegant; a full dress handkerchief, and
a bouquet of roses. 'Full gay, I think, for my *aunt.*'
That is true, Lucy, but nobody is old in Europe. I
was seated next the Duchess of Bedford, who had
a scarlet satin sack and coat, with a cushion full of
diamonds, for hair she has none, and is *but seventy-
six*, neither. Well, now for your cousin; a small,
white Leghorn hat, bound with pink satin ribbon;

a steel buckle and band which turned up at the side, and confined a large pink bow; large bow of the same kind of ribbon behind; a wreath of full-blown roses round the crown, and another of buds and roses withinside the hat, which being placed at the back of the hair brought the roses to the edge; you see it clearly; one red and black feather with two white ones, completed the head-dress. A gown and coat of Chambéri gauze, with a red satin stripe over a pink waist, and coat flounced with crape, trimmed with broad point and pink ribbon; wreaths of roses across the coat; gauze sleeves and ruffles."

Mrs. Adams was very fond of her nieces, and they must have their share of London finery. In July, 1786, she writes to "my dear girls":

"I bought me a blue sarcenet coat not long since; after making it up I found it was hardly wide enough to wear over a straw coat, but I thought it was no matter; I could send it to one of my nieces. When I went to put it up, I thought, I wished I had another. 'It is easily got,' said I. 'Ned, bring the carriage to the door and drive me to Thornton's, the petticoat shop.' 'Here, Madam, is a very nice pink coat, made too of the widest sarcenet.' 'Well, put it up.' So back I drove, and now, my dear girls, there is a coat for each of you. Settle between yourselves which shall have the blue and which the pink, pay no regard to the direction, only when you put them on, remember your aunt wishes they were better for your sakes."

Sarcenet was in those days "a fine soft silk," the word being "probably derived from 'Saracen.' " [1]

It is pleasant to fancy the delight of the nieces when the box from London arrived. How they shook out the shining folds and tried the coats on before the glass, and cried, "Dear, kind Aunt Abby!"

Though London claimed most of their time, there were pleasant jaunts now and then for the Adamses, to this or that famous place. They went to Windsor, to Bath (which Abigail disliked heartily), to Portsmouth. Mr. Adams' diary gives glimpses of some of these excursions:

"April, 1786. Edgehill and Worcester were curious and interesting to us, as scenes where freemen had fought for their rights. The people in the neighborhood appeared so ignorant and careless at Worcester, that I was provoked, and asked, 'And do Englishmen so soon forget the ground where liberty was fought for? Tell your neighbors and your children that this is holy ground; much holier

[1] "Concise Oxford Dictionary."

than that on which your churches stand. All England should come in pilgrimage to this hill once a year.'

"This animated them, and they seemed much pleased with it. Perhaps their awkwardness before might arise from their uncertainty of our sentiments concerning the civil wars."

A trip like this must have been a great refreshment to Mrs. Adams; she did not like London. She tells her friend, Mrs. Warren:

"I have resided in this country nearly two years, and, in that time, I have made some few acquaintances whom I esteem, and shall leave with regret; but the customs and manners of a metropolis are unfriendly to that social intercourse which I have ever been accustomed to. Amusement and diversion may always be purchased at the theatres and places of public resort, so that little pains are taken to cultivate that benevolence and interchange of kindness which sweetens life, in lieu of which mere visits of form are substituted to keep up the union. Not only the wrinkled brow of age is grasping at the card-table, and even tricking with mean avarice, but the virgin bloom of innocence and beauty is withered at the same vigils. I do not think I should draw a false picture of the nobility and gentry of this metropolis, if I were to assert that money and pleasure are the sole objects of their ardent pursuit; public virtue, and, indeed, all virtue, is exposed to sale, and as to principle, where is it to be found, either in the present administration or opposition? Luxury, dissipation, and vice, have a natural tendency to extirpate every generous principle, and leave the heart susceptible of the most malignant vices."

I think she longed for home throughout the three years of her stay in London. It was *not her own place*. She met many famous people, and was glad to meet them, but their ways were not her ways. Besides this, her reception at Court, as well as her husband's, had been as cold as policy and bare civility would allow. How could it be otherwise? How could George III, honest creature that he was, pretend to be glad to see the Minister of his own lost dominion? It was perhaps too much to expect of him, and Queen Charlotte was of no more heroic mold than he, of no more tact or innate courtesy, and behaved accordingly. Abigail Adams was too proud to allude to this at the time; there is no hint of it in the letters from London. It was not till long after this that in a letter to her daughter she shows something of the bitterness that still remained in her heart. It was when the French Revolution seemed to threaten disaster to the throne of England.

"Humiliation for Charlotte," she says, "is no sorrow for me. She richly deserves her full portion for the contempt and scorn which she took pains to discover."

Those must have been grave affronts indeed that made so deep and abiding an impression on a heart so good and kind.

The stay in London brought her two great joys: the happy marriage of her daughter Abigail to Colonel W. S. Smith, the young secretary of the American Legation, and the birth of her first grandson. But when all was said, it was a glad day that brought Mr. Adams' decision to petition Congress for leave to return home; and a far gladder one for Mrs. Adams, when she set foot once more, in May, 1788, on the shore of the country she so deeply loved.

CHAPTER XI

VEXATIOUS HONORS

WHILE the Adamses were still in England, the Constitution of the United States had been framed; had been signed, September 17th, 1787, by George Washington, as president of the convention charged with its preparation, and ratified by a majority of the States. Now, a few months after their return, the first Presidential election took place, and John Adams, after nominating George Washington for President, found himself by general consent elected Vice-President. He took the new honor quietly and seriously, as he took everything; nor is it likely that Mrs. Adams was unduly elated by it. They made little change in their sober way of life. We are told that "the town of Hartford could think of no gift so appropriate for John Adams on his way to be inaugurated Vice-President as a roll of cloth from its own looms. All true patriots heard with joy that . . . when the American Fabius stood forth to take the oath of office he was clad from head to foot in garments whose material was the product of the soil." But by the time John Adams was inaugurated President, he had advanced so far that he went to the ceremony in a coach and six, followed by a procession of coaches and four.

New York was then the seat of government, and it was near New York that Mr. Adams established his family. There were to be no more long separations, no weary leagues stretching between Portia and her dearest friend. Both of them longed for Braintree, the home of their hearts, but since both could not be there, neither would be. A suitable home was found at Richmond Hill, then a lovely country place, a mile and a half from New York, and here some pleasant months were passed. Mrs. Adams thus describes Richmond Hill to her sister:

"The house in which we reside is situated upon a hill, the avenue to which is interspersed with forest trees, under which a shrubbery rather too luxuriant and wild has taken shelter, owing to its having been deprived by death, some years since, of its original proprietor, who kept it in perfect order. In front of the house, the noble Hudson rolls his majestic waves, bearing upon his bosom innumerable small vessels, which are constantly forwarding the rich products of the neighboring soil to the busy hand of a more extensive commerce. Beyond the Hudson rises to our view the fertile country of the Jerseys, covered with a golden harvest, and pouring forth plenty like the cornucopiae of Ceres. On the right hand, an extensive plain presents us with a view of fields covered with verdure, and pastures full of cattle. On the left, the city opens upon us, intercepted only by clumps of trees, and some rising ground, which serves to heighten the beauty of the scene, by appearing to conceal a part. In the background is a large flower-garden, enclosed with a hedge and some very handsome trees. On one side of it, a grove of pines and oaks fit for contemplation. . . . If my days of fancy and romance were not past, I could find here an ample field for indulgence; yet, amidst these delightful scenes of nature, my heart pants for the society of my dear relatives and friends who are too far removed from me. . . ."

She was not long to enjoy the beauties of Richmond Hill. In 1790, the seat of government was transferred to Philadelphia, and thither the faithful pair journeyed. The change was a most uncomfortable, even a dangerous one for Mrs. Adams, who had barely recovered from a serious illness. Soon after her arrival (November 21, 1790), she writes to her daughter from her new abode:

"Bush Hill, as it is called, though by the way there remains neither bush nor shrub upon it, and very few trees, except the pine grove behind it,— yet Bush Hill is a very beautiful place. But the grand and sublime I left at Richmond Hill. The cultivation in sight and prospect are superior, but the Schuylkill is not more like the Hudson, than I to Hercules. The house is better finished within; but, when you come to compare the conveniences for storeroom, kitchen, closets, etc., there is nothing like it in the whole house. As chance governs many actions of my life, when we arrived in the city, we proceeded to the house. By accident, the vessel with our furniture had arrived the day before, and Briesler was taking in the first load into a house all green-painted, the workmen there with their brushes in hand. This was cold comfort in a house, where I suppose no fire had been kindled for several years, except in a back kitchen; but, as I expected many things of this kind, I was not disappointed nor discomfited. As no wood nor fodder had been provided before-hand, we could only turn about, and go to the City Tavern for the night.

"The next morning was pleasant, and I ventured to come up and take possession; but what confusion! Boxes, barrels, chairs, tables, trunks, etc.; every thing to be arranged, and few hands to accomplish it, for Briesler was obliged to be at the vessel. The first object was to get fires; the next to get up beds; but the cold, damp rooms, the new paint, etc., proved almost too much for me. On Friday we arrived here, and late on Saturday evening we got our furniture in. On Sunday, Thomas was laid up with rheumatism; on Monday, I was obliged to give Louisa an emetic; on Tuesday, Mrs. Briesler was taken with her old pain in her stomach; and, to complete the whole, on Thursday, Polly was seized with a violent pleuritic fever. She has been twice bled, a blister upon her side, and has not been out of bed since, only as she is taken up to have her bed made. And every day, the stormy ones excepted, from eleven until three, the house is filled with ladies and gentlemen. As all this is no more nor worse than I expected, I bear it without repining, and feel thankful that I have weathered it out without a relapse, though some days I have not been able to sit up. . . .

"I have not yet begun to return visits, as the ladies expect to find me at home, and I have not been in a state of health to do it; nor am I yet in a very eligible state to receive their visits. I, however, endeavored to have one room decent to receive them, which, with my own chamber, is as much as I can boast of at present being in tolerable order. The difficulty of getting workmen, Mr. Hamilton pleads as an excuse for the house not being ready. Mrs. Lear was in to see me yesterday, and assures me that I am much better off than Mrs. Washington will be when she arrives, for that their house is not likely to be completed this year. And, when all is done, it will not be Broadway. If New York wanted any revenge for the removal, the citizens might be glutted if they would come here, where every article has become almost double in price, and where it is not possible for Congress, and the appendages, to be half so well accommodated for a long time. One would suppose that the people thought Mexico was before them, and that Congress were the possessors."

This was indeed an ominous beginning of the winter. A week later Thomas, Mrs. Adams' third son, was taken very ill with rheumatic fever, the natural result of moving into a damp, unfinished house in November.

"It seems," writes the poor lady, "as if sickness

followed me wherever I go . . . I had a great misfortune happen to my best trunk of clothes. The vessel sprunk a leak, and my trunk got wet a foot high, by which means I have several gowns spoiled; and the one you worked is the most damaged, and a black satin;—the blessed effects of tumbling about the world."

A month later, things were scarcely better.

"I would tell you that I had an ague in my face, and a violent toothache, which has prevented my writing to you all day; but I am determined to brave it out this evening, and enquire how you do. Without further complaint, I have become so tender, from keeping so much in a warm chamber, that, as soon as I set my feet out, I am sure to come home with some new pain or ache."

Philadelphia was gay that winter: a "constellation of beauties" was sparkling in the social firmament. Mrs. Adams cannot say enough about "the dazzling Mrs. Bingham," who "has certainly given laws to the ladies here, in fashion and elegance: their manners and appearance are superior to what I have seen." She adds: "I should spend a very dissipated winter, if I were to accept one-half the invitations I receive, particularly to the routs, or tea and cards. Even Saturday evening is not excepted, and I refused an invitation of that kind for this evening. I have been to one assembly. The dancing was very good; the company of the best kind. The President and Madam, the Vice-President and Madam, Ministers of State, and their Madams, etc.; but the room despicable; the etiquette,—it was difficult to say where it was to be found."

She is writing to Mrs. Smith, the beloved daughter whom she missed daily and hourly. In this same letter (January 8th 1791) we catch a glimpse of the Vice-President which would have astonished his fellow-workers in Congress. Little John Smith was visiting his grandparents at this time. "As to John," says Grandmother Abigail, "we grow every day fonder of him. He has spent an hour this afternoon in driving his grandpapa round the room with a willow stick."

I shall never again see a portrait of John Adams, dignified and portly, in powder and pigtail, without calling up this pleasant companion picture of the grandfather capering about the room to the whistling of a willow switch.

The following letters, written by Mr. Adams while on a visit to Quincy, show him in his most delightful aspect.

"You apologize for the length of your letters,

and I ought to excuse the shortness and emptiness of mine. Yours give me more entertainment than all the speeches I hear. There are more good thoughts, fine strokes, and mother wit in them than I hear in the whole week. An ounce of mother wit is worth a pound of clergy; and I rejoice that one of my children, at least, has an abundance of not only mother wit, but his mother's wit. It is one of the most amiable and striking traits in his composition. It appeared in all its glory and severity in 'Barneveldt.'

"If the rogue has any family pride, it is all derived from the same source. His Pa renounces and abjures every trace of it. He has curiosity to know his descent and comfort in the knowledge that his ancestors, on both sides, for several generations, have been innocent. But no pride in this. Pomp, splendor, office, title, power, riches are the sources of pride, but even these are not excuse for pride. The virtues and talents of ancestors should be considered as examples and solemn trusts and produce meekness, modesty, and humility, lest they should not be imitated and equalled. Mortification and humiliation can be the only legitimate feelings of a mind conscious that it falls short of its ancestors in merit. I must stop."

"You say so many handsome things to me, re-specting my letters, that you ought to fear making me vain; since, however we may appreciate the encomiums of the world, the praises of those whom we love and esteem are more dangerous, because we are led to believe them the most sincere. . . .

"Prince Edward sailed last Saturday. He sent his aides to visit the Lieutenant-Governor, but would not go himself. He dined with Mrs. Han-cock, and was visited by many gentlemen in town. He went to the assembly with Mr. Russell, and danced with Mrs. Russell. He went to visit the college, but I did not hear that he had any curi-osity to see Bunker Hill. He related an anecdote at the table of the English consul. As he was coming from Quebec, he stopped at an inn, where an elderly countryman desired to see him. After some bow-ing, etc., the countryman said: 'I hear you are King George's son.' 'They tell me so,' said the prince. 'And, pray how do you like this country?' 'Why, very well,' replied his highness. 'And how do you think your father liked to lose it?' 'Why, not half so well as I should like to live in it,' replied the prince, which answer pleased the countryman. I hear he took notice of all the French refugees, and offered any of them a passage with him to the West

Indies. His stay here was very short, and it was best it should be so."

One has pleasant glimpses of George Washington, in Mrs. Adams' letters. One day she dined with him and Mrs. Washington and found him "more than usually social. . . . He asked very affectionately after you and the children, and at table picked the sugar-plums from a cake, and requested me to take them for master John."

The custom of sending bonbons to the children dates back to Colonial times, when any social entertainment was apt to be followed by what was pleasantly called "Cold Party." The day after, the hostess would send a judicious assortment of left-over delicacies to such neighbors as had been unable to join the party. In my own childhood, my mother's going to a dinner party was always an occasion of excitement, because of wonderful bonbons that we children would receive the next day; pieces of red or white sugar candy, in elaborate wrappings of gilt paper, tinsel and gauze: I do not see the like today.

Philadelphia society was certainly brilliant in those days. The Duke of Rochefoucauld-Liancourt was deeply impressed by it, and wrote in his book of Travels:

"The profusion and luxury of Philadelphia on great days, at the tables of the wealthy, in their equipages, and the dresses of their wives and daughters, are, as I have observed, extreme. I have seen balls on the President's birthday where the splendor of the rooms, and the variety and richness of the dresses did not suffer in comparison with Europe; and it must be acknowledged that the beauty of the American ladies has the advantage in the comparison. The young women of Philadelphia are accomplished in different degrees, but beauty is general with them. They want the ease and fashion of Frenchwomen; but the brilliancy of their complexion is infinitely superior. Even when they grow old they are still handsome; and it would be no exaggeration to say in the numerous assemblies of Philadelphia it is impossible to meet with what is called a plain woman. As for the young men, they for the most part seem to belong to another species."

What were these rich and various dresses? We have chapter and verse for some of them. One lady wore at a certain ball "a plain celestial-blue satin, with a white satin petticoat. On the neck was worn a very large Italian gauze handkerchief, with border stripes of satin. The head-dress was a pouf of gauze, in the form of a globe, the creneaux or head-piece of which was composed of white satin, having a double wing in large plaits, and trimmed with a wreath of artificial roses, falling from the left at the top to the right at the bottom, in front, and the reverse behind. The hair was dressed all over in detached curls, four of which, in two ranks, fell on each side of the neck, and were relieved behind by a floating *chignon*."

The gentleman who led this gorgeous costume and its wearer through "Sir Roger de Coverley" was doubtless dressed in more sober fashion. One of these republican exquisites thus describes his own costume, possibly at the same ball: "I was dressed in a light French blue coat, with a high collar, broad lappels, and large gilt buttons, a double-breasted Marseilles vest, Nankeen-colored cassimere breeches, with white silk stockings, shining pumps, and full ruffles on my breast and at my wrists, to-gether with a ponderous white cravat, with a pud-ding in it, as we then called it; and I was consid-ered the best dressed gentleman in the room."

The winter of 1790-91 was one of extremes. The Adamses burned forty cords of wood in four months. On the 17th and 18th of March, Mrs. Adams dined with all the windows open, put out the fires, and "ate ice to cool her; the glasses at 80." On the 20th, it snowed all day, the snow followed by a keen northwester and frost. In bad weather it was difficult for the dwellers at Bush Hill to stir from their abode.

"We are only two miles from town, yet have I been more of a prisoner this winter than I ever was in my life. The road from hence to the pavement is one mile and a half, the soil a brick clay, so that, when there has been heavy rain, or a thaw, you must wallow to the city through a bed of mortar without a bottom, the horses sinking to their knees. If it becomes cold, then the holes and the roughness are intolerable."

The next published letter of Mrs. Adams is dated Quincy, 11 February, 1793. It is to Mrs. Smith, and is largely concerned with political issues which today have lost their poignancy. She has much to say of the "artifices and lies of the Jacobins," meaning the anti-Federalist party, which was opposed to Washington and Adams. It is strange indeed to read today that "the President has been openly abused in the *National Gazette,*—abused for his levees as an ape of royalty; Mrs. Washington abused for her drawing-rooms; their celebration of birth-days sneered at; himself insulted because he has not come forward and exerted his influence in favor of a further compensation to the army. They even tell him that a greater misfortune cannot befall a people than for their President to have no competitor; that it infuses into him a supercilious spirit, renders him self-important, and creates an idea that one man only is competent to govern. They compare him to a hyena and a crocodile; charge him with duplicity and deception. The President has not been accustomed to such language, and his feelings will be wounded, I presume."

I presume they were. Nobody likes to be called a hyena and a crocodile, and *Pater Patriae* could not fail to be sensible of a lack of propriety in the epithets.

It was all natural enough, perhaps. These were the days of the French Revolution, and all the world was heaving with the throes of that tremendous convulsion. We were fortunate to get nothing worse than a little recrimination, which did no lasting harm. We are ignorant of the names of those who called Washington hyena and crocodile, and we have no curiosity on the subject.

Neither President nor Vice-President had much comfort in their second term. The political pot was seething furiously; men were burning their fingers, and crying out with pain of the burning. "Envy, hatred, malice, and all uncharitableness" ran rife in the Republic where brotherly love should rule in peace. Six months before the end of his second term, Washington announced his resolve to retire from public service; a resolve not to be shaken by any entreaties. By this time the country, which had stood united through the first Presidential election, and divided only on the minor issue (the choice of a Vice-President), in the second was definitely split into two factions: Federalists and Democratic-Republicans faced each other in ardent strife. As I have said before, I am not writing a history: suffice it to say that John Adams, as Federalist candidate, was elected President, his rival, Thomas Jefferson, becoming Vice-President.

Mrs. Adams' letter to her husband on the day of his inauguration, February 8th, 1797, has become a classic, and is in every way worthy of her.

> "The sun is dressed in brightest beams,
> To give thy honors to the day.

"And may it prove an auspicious prelude to each ensuing season. You have this day to declare yourself head of a nation. 'And now, O Lord, my God, thou hast made thy servant ruler over the people.

Give unto him an understanding heart, that he may know how to go out and come in before this great people; that he may discern between good and bad. For who is able to judge this thy so great a people?' were the words of a royal sovereign; and not less applicable to him who is invested with the chief magistracy of a nation, though he wear not a crown, nor the robes of royalty.

"My thoughts and my meditations are with you, though personally absent; and my petitions to Heaven are, that 'the things which make for peace may not be hidden from your eyes.' My feelings are not those of pride or ostentation, upon the occasion. They are solemnized by a sense of the obligations, the important trusts, and numerous duties connected with it. That you may be enabled to discharge them with honor to yourself, with justice and impartiality to your country, and with satisfaction to this great people, shall be the daily prayer of your

"A. A."

Philadelphia was still the seat of government, the new city of Washington not being yet ready for occupation. There are few published letters of this period; the cares and calls of society were heavy upon Mrs. Adams. She had never fully recovered from the illness of 1790, and was subject to recurrent attacks of fever. She spent as much of her time as was possible at Quincy, the name now given to that part of Braintree where they lived. When in Philadelphia, and later in Washington, she performed the duties of her high office carefully, thoroughly, with her own stately dignity, but I doubt if she ever enjoyed them. She writes to her friend, Mrs. James Warren, on March 4th, 1797:

"For your congratulations upon a late important event accept my acknowledgments. Considering it as the voluntary and unsolicited gift of a free and enlightened people, it is a precious and valuable deposit and calls for every exertion of the head and every virtue of the heart to do justice to so sacred a trust. Yet, however pure the intentions or upright the conduct, offences will come,

High stations tumult but not bliss create.

"As to a crown, my dear Madam, I will not deny that there is one which I aspire after, and in a country where envy can never enter to plant thorns beneath it. The fashion of this world passeth away— I would hope that I have not lived in vain, but have learnt how to estimate and what value to place upon the fleeting and transitory enjoyment of it. I shall

esteem myself peculiarly fortunate, if, at the close
of my public life, I can retire esteemed, beloved and
equally respected with my predecessor."

Mr. Adams' feelings are expressed in the following words, written to his wife the day after the
election.

"Your dearest friend never had a more trying
day than yesterday. A solemn scene it was indeed,
and it was made more affecting to me by the presence of the General, whose countenance was as se-
rene and unclouded as the day. He seemed to me to
enjoy a triumph over me. Methought I heard him
say, 'Ay! I am fairly out, and you are fairly in!
See which of us will be happiest.' When the ceremony was over, he came and made me a visit, and
cordially congratulated me, and wished my administration might be happy, successful and honorable."

There were thorns enough in the presidential
"crown," for both Mr. and Mrs. Adams. The
storm, instead of abating, rose higher and higher.
There was danger of war with France : a danger
only averted by the rise of Napoleon Bonaparte to
power, as First Consul of France. Consequent upon
these troubles came the Alien and Sedition Acts,
which brought endless vexation of spirit for President Adams and for everyone else concerned in

them. The details of the struggle may not be given here: suffice it to say that through four tempestuous years the old statesman fought gallantly and steadfastly for the political principles which were dearer to him than life itself, but fought in vain. The tide had set against him, and in November, 1800, he had the intense mortification of seeing his colleague, his former friend and present rival, Thomas Jefferson, elected President in his place.

This was bitter indeed to the stout patriot who had given his whole life to the service of his country. Conscious of his absolute integrity ("He is vain and irritable," said Jefferson himself, "but disinterested as the being who made him!"), and his unfailing devotion, John Adams could not but resent the slight put upon him; nor, strive as she might, could his faithful Portia help resenting it for him. She writes to her son Thomas (November 13th, 1800):

"Well, my dear son, South Carolina has behaved as your father always said she would. The consequence to us, personally, is, that we retire from public life. For myself and family, I have few regrets. At my age, and with my bodily infirmities, I shall be happier at Quincy. Neither my habits, nor my education, or inclinations have led me to an expensive style of living, so that on that score I have little to mourn over. If I did not rise with dignity, I can at least fall with ease, which is the more difficult task. I wish your father's circumstances were not so limited and circumscribed, as they must be, because he cannot indulge himself in those improvements upon his farm, which his inclination leads him to, and which would serve to amuse him, and contribute to his health. I feel not any resentment against those who are coming into power, and only wish the future administration of the government may be as productive of the peace, happiness, and prosperity of the nation, as the two former ones have been. I leave to time the unfolding of a drama. I leave to posterity to reflect upon the times past; and I leave them characters to contemplate. My own intention is to return to Quincy as soon as I conveniently can; I presume in the month of January."

It was at this trying time that the seat of government was transferred to Washington. What the President's wife thought of the move is apparent from the following letters to her daughter:

"I arrived here on Sunday last, and without meeting with any accident worth noticing, except losing ourselves when we left Baltimore, and going eight or nine miles on the Frederick road, by which means we were obliged to go the other eight through woods, where we wandered two hours without finding a guide, or the path.   Fortunately, a straggling black came up with us, and we engaged him as a guide, to extricate us out of our difficulty; but woods are all you see, from Baltimore until you reach *the city,* which is only so in name.   Here and there is a small cot, without a glass window, interspersed amongst the forests, through which you travel miles without seeing any human being.   In the city there are buildings enough, if they were compact and finished, to accommodate Congress and those attached to it; but as they are, and scattered as they are, I see no great comfort for them.   The river, which runs up to Alexandria, is in full view of my window, and I see the vessels as they pass and repass.   The house is upon a grand and superb scale, requiring about thirty servants to attend and keep the apartments in proper order, and perform the ordinary business of the house and stables; an establishment very well proportioned to the President's salary.   The lighting the apartments, from the kitchen to parlors and chambers, is a tax indeed; and the fires we are obliged to keep to secure us from daily agues is another very cheering comfort.

SOUTH ELEVATION OF THE PRESIDENT'S HOUSE

Copied from the design of proposed alterations, 1807

To assist us in this great castle, and render less attendance necessary, bells are wholly wanting, not one single one being hung through the whole house, and promises are all you can obtain. This is so great an inconvenience, that I know not what to do, or how to do. The ladies from Georgetown and in the city have many of them visited me. Yesterday I returned fifteen visits,—but such a place as Georgetown appears,—why, our Milton is beautiful. But no comparisons;—if they will put me up some bells, and let me have wood enough to keep fires, I design to be pleased. I could content myself almost anywhere three months; but, surrounded with forests, can you believe that wood is not to be had, because people cannot be found to cut and cart it! Briesler entered into a contract with a man to supply him with wood. A small part, a few cords only, has he been able to get. Most of that was expended to dry the walls of the house before we came in, and yesterday the man told him it was impossible for him to procure it to be cut and carted. He has had recourse to coals; but we cannot get grates made and set. We have, indeed, come into *a new country*.

"You must keep all this to yourself, and, when asked how I like it, say that I write you the situation is beautiful, which is true. The house is made habitable, but there is not a single apartment finished, and all withinside, except the plastering, has been done since Briesler came. We have not the least fence, yard, or other convenience, without, and the great unfinished audience-room I make a drying-room of, to hang up the clothes in. The principal stairs are not up, and will not be this winter. Six chambers are made comfortable; two are occupied by the President and Mr. Shaw; two lower rooms, one for a common parlor, and one for a levee-room. Up stairs there is the oval room, which is designed for the drawing-room, and has the crimson furniture in it. It is a very handsome room now; but, when completed, it will be beautiful. If the twelve years, in which this place has been considered as the future seat of government, had been improved, as they would have been if in New England, very many of the present inconveniences would have been removed. It is a beautiful spot, capable of every improvement, and, the more I view it, the more I am delighted with it."

"27 November, 1800.

"I received your letter by Mr. Pintard. Two articles we are much distressed for; the one is bells, but the more important one is wood. Yet you cannot see wood for trees. No arrangement has been made, but by promises never performed, to supply the new-comers with fuel. Of the promises Briesler has received his full share. He had procured nine cords of wood; between six and seven of that was kindly burnt up to dry the walls of the house, which ought to have been done by the commissioners, but which, if left to them, would have remained undone to this day. Congress poured in, but shiver, shiver. No woodcutters nor carters to be had at any rate. We are now indebted to a Pennsylvania waggon to bring us, through the first clerk in the Treasury office, one cord and a half of wood, which is all we have for this house, where twelve fires are constantly required, and where, we are told, the roads will soon be so bad that it cannot be drawn. Briesler procured two hundred bushels of coals or we must have suffered. This is the situation of almost every person. The public officers have sent to Philadelphia for woodcutters and waggons.

"You will read in the answer of the House to the President's Speech a full and explicit approbation of the Administration; a coöperation with him equal to his utmost expectations; this passed with-

out an amendment or any debate or squabble, and
has just now been delivered by the House in a body.
The vessel which has my clothes and other matters
is not arrived. The ladies are impatient for a
drawing-room; I have no looking-glasses but
dwarfs for this house; nor a twentieth part lamps
enough to light it. Many things were stolen, many
more broken, by the removal; amongst the number,
my tea china is more than half missing. Georgetown affords nothing. My rooms are very pleasant and warm whilst the doors of the hall are
closed.

"You can scarce believe that here in this wilderness city, I should find my time so occupied as it
is. My visitors, some of them, come three and
four miles. The return of one of them is the work
of one day; most of the ladies reside in Georgetown or in scattered parts of the city at two and
three miles distance. Mrs. Otis, my nearest neigh-
bour, is at lodgings almost half a mile from me;
Mrs. Senator Otis, two miles.

"We have all been very well as yet; if we can by
any means get wood, we shall not let our fires go
out, but it is at a price indeed; from four dollars
it has risen to nine. Some say it will fall, but there

must be more industry than is to be found here to
bring half enough to the market for the consump-
tion of the inhabitants.

"With kind remembrance to all friends,

"I am your truly affectionate mother,

"A. A."

John Cotton Smith, Member of Congress from
Connecticut, adds these details:

"One wing of the Capitol only had been erected,
which with the President's House, a mile distant
from it, both constructed with white sandstone, were
striking objects in dismal contrast with the scene
around them.   Instead of recognizing the avenues
and streets, pourtrayed on the plan of the city, not
one was visible, unless we except a road with two
buildings on each side of it, called the New Jersey
Avenue. The Pennsylvania, leading, as laid down
on paper, from the Capitol to the Presidential Mansion, was then nearly the whole distance a deep
morass, covered with alder bushes, which were cut
through the width of the intended avenue the then
ensuing winter. . . . The roads in every direction
were muddy and unimproved; a sidewalk was attempted in one instance by a covering formed of
the chips of the stones which had been hewed from

the Capitol. It extended but a little way, and was of little value, for in dry weather the sharp fragments cut our shoes, and in wet weather covered them with white mortar."

Mrs. Adams was to have only four months of this disturbed existence. The climate of Washington, the general discomfort added to anxiety and distress of mind, made her ill, and she left the city before Mr. Adams did. During her short stay, however, she won the admiration of all by the dignity, grace and judgment with which she filled a most difficult position. She *never lost her cheerfulness*. "I am a mortal enemy," she said, "to anything but a cheerful countenance and a merry heart, which Solomon tells us, does good like a medicine." So in those dark days, when the tide of abuse and calumny raged around her beloved husband, she was more than ever the lamp that lighted and the fire that warmed him. Whatever was said of him —and one fancies that "hyena" and "crocodile" were mild epithets compared with those showered on the brave old statesman,—no one had anything but praise for Mrs. Adams. On January 1st, 1801, was held the first New Year's reception at the White House. She received the guests with her own calm grace and dignity. No one would have guessed that the house was half finished, the principal stairs still lacking, her china stolen and her husband defeated; she was mistress, not only of the White House, but of the situation.

The closing days of the winter must have been painful to both Mr. and Mrs. Adams. They longed for the end, for the permanent return to "calm, happy Braintree," and before March came, Mrs. Adams was already there, ready to receive her dearest friend. One of Mr. Adams' last acts was the appointment of John Marshall as chief-justice of the supreme court; for this alone, he would deserve the lasting gratitude of the American people. He could not meet Jefferson, whom he had once loved, with whom he had toiled, suffered, triumphed, by whom he was now defeated. On March 3rd, 1801, he labored far into the night, signing commissions, arranging papers in his own methodical way, closing, as it were, his accounts with a nation which he could not but think ungrateful. Early on the morning of the 4th, while the city was still wrapped in slumber, he entered his carriage and left Washington forever.

CHAPTER XII

AFTERNOON AND EVENING

IT was not in the little "hut" of former days that Portia awaited her dearest friend. A statelier dwelling was theirs henceforth, the house built by Leonard Vassall, a West India planter. It stood, and still stands, in its ample grounds, under its branching elms. The original building has received many additions, but it is the same house to which John Adams came on that spring day of 1801; the home of his later life, and of three generations of his descendants.

John Adams was now sixty-six years old, still in the fullness of vigorous manhood. I seem to see him entering that door, a defeated and disappointed man, yet holding his head as high, and looking forward with as clear and steadfast a gaze as if he were come home in triumph. He might be angry, he might be hurt; but no injury could bow the head, or bend the broad shoulders, of him who had once been acclaimed as the Atlas of Independence. Thus seeing him, I cannot but recall the summing up of his character by another strong man, Theodore Parker, the preacher.

"The judgment of posterity will be, that he was a brave man, deep-sighted, conscientious, patriotic, and possessed of Integrity which nothing ever shook, but which stood firm as the granite of his Quincy Hills. While American Institutions continue, the People will honor *brave, honest old John Adams,* who never failed his country in her hour of need, and who, in his life of more than ninety years, though both passionate and ambitious, wronged no man nor any woman.

"And all the people shall say Amen!"

In this peaceful and pleasant home, Mr. and Mrs. Adams were to pass the rest of their days. They wasted no time in repining; they were thankful to be at home, eager to enjoy the fruits of leisure and the quiet mind. By early May, Mrs. Adams was setting out raspberry bushes and strawberry vines, and working daily in her dairy. She sends word to her daughter that she might see her at five o'clock in the morning, skimming her milk.

She was not the only busy one. "You will find your father," she writes to her son Thomas, "in his fields, attending to his hay-makers. . . . The crops of hay have been abundant; upon this spot, where eight years ago we cut scarcely six tons, we now have thirty."

Mr. Josiah Quincy, in his "Figures of the Past," gives us delightful glimpses of Mr. and Mrs. Adams. He was a child of five when he used to gaze in wonder at the second President in Quincy meetinghouse.

"The President's pew was conspicuous in the reconstructed edifice, and there the old man was to be seen at every service. An air of respectful deference to John Adams seemed to pervade the building. The ministers brought their best sermons when they came to exchange, and had a certain consciousness in their manner, as if officiating before royalty. The medley of stringed and wind instruments in the gallery—a survival of the sacred trumpets and shawms mentioned by King David—seemed to the imagination of a child to be making discord together in honor of the venerable chief who was the centre of interest."

As Josiah Quincy recalls his childhood, so the old President loved to recall his own. "I shall never forget," he would say, "the rows of venerable heads ranged along those front benches which, as a young fellow, I used to gaze upon. They were as old and gray as mine is now."

When he was six, Josiah Quincy was put to school to the Reverend Peter Whitney, and, while there, was often asked to dine at the Adams house of a Sunday. "This was at first," he says, "somewhat of an ordeal for a boy; but the genuine kindness of the President, who had not the smallest chip of an iceberg in his composition, soon made me perfectly at ease in his society." With Mrs. Adams, he found "a shade more formality"; but this wore off, and he became much attached to her. "She always dressed handsomely, and her rich silks and laces seemed appropriate to a lady of her dignified position in the town." He adds:

"I well remember the modest dinner at the President's, to which I brought a school-boy's appetite. The pudding, generally composed of boiled corn-meal, always constituted the first course. This was the custom of the time,—it being thought desirable to take the edge off one's hunger before reaching the joint. Indeed, it was considered wise to stimulate the young to fill themselves with pudding, by the assurance that the boy who managed to eat the most of it should be helped most abundantly to the meat, which was to follow. It need not be said that neither the winner nor his competitors found much room for meat at the close of their contest; and so the domestic economy of the arrangement was very apparent. Miss Smith, a niece of Mrs. Adams, was an inmate of the President's family, and one of these ladies always carved. Mr. Adams made his contribution to the service of the table in the form of that good-humoured, easy banter, which makes a dinner of herbs more digestible than is a stalled ox without it. At a late period of our acquaintance, I find preserved in my journals frequent though too meagre reports of his conversation. But of the time of which I am writing there is not a word discoverable. I can distinctly picture to myself a certain iron spoon which the old gentleman once fished up from the depths of a pudding in which it had been unwittingly cooked; but of the pleasant things he said in those easy dinner-talks no trace remains."

Henry Bradshaw Fearon, an Englishman who visited the Adamses in 1817, gives this description of the dinner:

"1st course a pudding made of Indian corn, molasses and butter. 2nd, veal, bacon, neck of mutton, potatoes, cabbages, carrots and Indian beans, Madeira wine, of which each drank two glasses. We

sat down to dinner at one o'clock. At two nearly
all went a second time to church. For tea we had
pound cake, wheat bread and butter, and bread made
out of Indian corn and rye. Tea was brought from
the kitchen and handed round by a neat white servant girl. The topics of conversation were various:
England, America, politics, literature, science and
Dr. Priestley, Miss Edgeworth, Mrs. Siddons, Mr.
Kean, France, Shakespeare, Moore, Lord Byron,
Cobbett, American Revolution, the traitor, Gen. Ar-
nold. . . . The establishment of the political pa-
triarch consists of a house two stories high, containing, I believe, eight rooms; of two men and
three maidservants, three horses and a plain carriage."

Mrs. Adams' strength continued to decline,
though her spirits never flagged. She writes to her
sister, Mrs. Shaw, in June, 1809:

"I was unable to reply to my dear sister's letter
of May 19th when I received it, being visited by St.
Anthony, who scourged me most cruelly. I am sure
I wished well to the Spanish patriots, in their late
struggle for liberty, and I bore no ill-will to those
whose tutelar saint, thus unprovoked, beset me. I
wish he had been preaching to the fishes, who, according to tradition, have been his hearers; for so

ill did he use me, that I came near losing my senses. I think he must be a very bigoted saint, a favorer of the Inquisition, and a tyrant. If such are the penances of saints, I hope to hold no further intercourse with them. For four days and nights my face was so swelled and inflamed, that I was almost blind. It seemed as though my blood boiled. Until the third day, when I sent for the doctor, I knew not what the matter was. It confined me for ten days. My face is yet red; but I rode out today, and feel much better. I think a little journey would be of service to me; but I find, as years and infirmities increase, my courage and enterprise diminish. Ossian says, 'Age is dark and unlovely.' When I look in my glass, I do not much wonder at the story related of a very celebrated painter, Zeuxis, who, it is said, died of laughing at a comical picture he had made of an old woman. If our glass flatters us in youth, it tells us truths in age. The cold hand of death has frozen up some of the streams of our early friendships; the congelation is gaining upon vital powers and marking us for the tomb. 'May we so number our days as to apply our hearts unto wisdom.'

"The man is yet unborn, who duly weighs an hour.

"When my family was young around me, I used to find more leisure, and think I could leave it with less anxiety than I can now. There is not any occasion for detailing the whys and wherefores. It is said, if riches increase, those increase that eat them; but what shall we say, when the eaters increase without the wealth? You know, my dear sister, if there be bread enough, and to spare, unless a prudent attention manage that sufficiency, the fruits of diligence will be scattered by the hand of dissipation. No man ever prospered in the world without the consent and coöperation of his wife. It behoves us, who are parents or grandparents, to give our daughters and granddaughters, when their education devolves upon us, such an education as shall qualify them for the useful and domestic duties of life, that they should learn the proper use and improvement of time, since 'time was given for use, not waste.' The finer accomplishments, such as music, dancing, and painting, serve to set off and embellish the picture; but the groundwork must be formed of more durable colors.

"I consider it as an indispensable requisite, that every American wife should herself know how to order and regulate her family; how to govern her domestics, and train up her children. For this pur-

pose, the all-wise Creator made woman an help-meet
for man, and she who fails in these duties does not
answer the end of her creation.

> Life's cares are comforts; such by Heaven designed;
> They that have none must make them, or be wretched.
> Cares are employments, and, without employ,
> The soul is on a rack, the rack of rest.

I have frequently said to my friends, when they
have thought me overburdened with cares, I would
rather have too much than too little. Life stag-
nates without action. I could never bear merely to
vegetate;

> Waters stagnate when they cease to flow."

Some of the most delightful letters of her later
years are addressed to her granddaughter, Caroline
Smith. The two following ones give a lively picture of her daily life.

"Your letter, my dear Caroline, gave me pleasure. As all yours are calculated to enliven the spirits, I take them as a cordial, which during the resi-
dence of the bald-pated winter and a close confine-
ment to my chamber for several weeks, I have been
much in want of. And now what return can I make
you? What can you expect from age, debility and
weakness?

"Why, you shall have the return of a grateful

heart, which amidst infirmities is not insensible to the many blessings which encompass it. Food, raiment and fuel, dear and kind friends and relatives, mental food and entertainment sufficient to satisfy the craving appetite, and the hopes and prospect of another and better country, even an heavenly.

> Eternal power! from whom these blessings flow,
> Teach me still more to wonder—more to know,
> Here round my home still lift my soul to thee,
>
> And let me ever midst thy bounties raise
> An humble note of thankfulness and praise.

"Although my memory is not so tenacious as in youth, nor my eye-sight so clear, my hearing is unimpaired, my heart warm and my affections are as fervent to those in whom 'my days renew' as formerly to those from 'whom my days I drew.' I have some troubles in the loss of friends by death, and no small solicitude for the motherless offspring, but my trust and confidence are in that being who 'hears the young ravens when they cry.' I do not know, my dear Caroline, that I ever gave you encouragement to expect me at the valley, although I should rejoice to be able to visit you—but I now look forward with the hope of seeing you here as an attendant upon your mother as soon as the spring opens and the roads will permit.

"We have snow by the cargo this winter. Not a bird flits but a hungry crow now and then, in quest of prey. The fruit trees exhibit a mournful picture, broken down by the weight of the snow; whilst the running of sleighs and the jingle of bells assures us that all nature does not slumber.

"As if you love me, proverbially, you must love my dog, you will be glad to learn that Juno yet lives, although like her mistress she is gray with age. She appears to enjoy life and to be grateful for the attention paid her. She wags her tail and announces a visitor whenever one appears.

"Adieu, my dear child—remember me with affection to your brother and with kind affection to your honored father and also to your uncle whose benevolent qualities I respect and whose cheerful spirits have made 'the wilderness to smile and blossom as the rose.'   Most affectionately,

"Your Grandmother,
"ABIGAIL ADAMS."

"Quincy, 19 November, 1812.
"MY DEAR CAROLINE:

"Your neat, pretty letter, looking small, but containing much, reached me this day. I have a good mind to give you the journal of the day.

"Six o'clock. Rose, and, in imitation of his Britannic Majesty, kindled my own fire. Went to the stairs, as usual, to summon George and Charles. Returned to my chamber, dressed myself. No one stirred. Called a second time, with a voice a little raised.

"Seven o'clock. Blockheads not out of bed. Girls in motion. Mean, when I hire another manservant, that he shall come for *one call*.

"Eight o'clock. Fires made, breakfast prepared. L—— in Boston. Mrs. A. at the tea-board. Forgot the sausages. Susan's recollection brought them upon the table.

"*Enter* Ann. 'Ma'am, the man is come with coals.'

"'Go, call George to assist him.' (*Exit* Ann.)

"*Enter* Charles. 'Mr. B—— is come with cheese, turnips, etc. Where are they to be put?' 'I will attend to him myself.' (*Exit* Charles.)

"Just seated at the table again.

"*Enter* George with, 'Ma'am, here is a man with a drove of pigs.' A consultation is held upon this important subject, the result of which is the purchase of two spotted swine.

"Nine o'clock. *Enter* Nathaniel, from the upper house, with a message for sundries; and black

Thomas's daughter, for sundries. Attended to all these concerns. A little out of sorts that I could not finish my breakfast. Note: never to be incommoded with trifles.

"*Enter* George Adams, from the post-office,—a large packet from Russia,[1] and from the valley also. Avaunt, all cares,—I put you all aside,—and thus I find good news from a far country,—children, grandchildren, all well. I had no expectation of hearing from Russia this winter, and the pleasure was the greater to obtain letters of so recent a date, and to learn that the family were all in health. For this blessing give I thanks.

"At twelve o'clock, by a previous engagement, I was to call at Mr. G——'s for Cousin B. Smith to accompany me to the bridge at Quincy-port, being the first day of passing it. The day was pleasant; the scenery delightful. Passed both bridges, and entered Hingham. Returned before three o'clock. Dined, and,

"At five, went to Mr. T. G——'s, with your grandfather; the third visit he has made with us in *the week;* and let me whisper to you he played at whist with Mr. J. G——, who was as ready and

[1] John Quincy Adams was at this time Ambassador at St. Petersburg.

accurate as though he had both eyes to see with. Returned.

"At nine, sat down and wrote a letter.

"At eleven, retired to bed. We do not so every week. I tell it you as one of the marvels of the age. By all this, you will learn that grandmother has got rid of her croaking, and that grandfather is in good health, and that both of us are as tranquil as that bald old fellow, called Time, will let us be.

"And here I was interrupted in my narrative.

"I re-assume my pen upon the 22d of November, being this day sixty-eight years old. How many reflections occur to me upon this anniversary!

"What have I done for myself or others in this long period of my sojourn, that I can look back upon with pleasure, or reflect upon with approbation? Many, very many follies and errors of judgment and conduct rise up before me, and ask forgiveness of that Being, who seeth into the secret recesses of the heart, and from whom nothing is hidden. I think I may with truth say, that in no period of my life have the vile passions had control over me. I bear no enmity to any human being; but, alas! as Mrs. Placid said to her friend, by which of thy good works wouldst thou be willing to be judged? I do not believe, with some divines, that all our good works are but as filthy rags; the example which our great Master has set before us, of purity, benevolence, obedience, submission and humility, are virtues which, if faithfully practised, will find their reward; or why has he pronounced so many benedictions upon them in his sermon on the mount? I would ask with the poet,

> Is not virtue in mankind
> The nutriment that feeds the mind,
> Then who, with reason, can pretend
> That all effects of virtue end?

I am one of those who are willing to rejoice always. My disposition and habits are not of the gloomy kind. I believe that 'to enjoy is to obey.'

> Yet not to Earth's contracted span,
>   Thy goodness let me bound;
> Or think thee Lord alone of man,
>   Whilst thousand worlds are round."

This period of quiet retirement did not lack its thrills of interest, public and private. Europe was in the throes of the Napoleonic Wars, a conflict surpassed in bitterness only by that of our own day. In due time came our own War of 1812, and for three years this country was in a continual state of alarm. On December 30th, 1812, Mrs. Adams writes to her friend of many years, Mrs. Mercy Warren:

"So long as we are inhabitants of this earth and possess any of our faculties, we cannot be indifferent to the state of our country, our posterity and our friends. Personally we have arrived so near the close of the drama that we can experience but few of the evils which await the rising generation. We have passed through one revolution and have happily arrived at the goal, but the ambition, injustice and plunder of foreign powers have again involved us in war, the termination of which is not given us to see.

"If we have not 'the gorgeous palaces of the cloud-capp'd towers' of Moscow to be levelled with the dust, nor a million of victims to sacrifice upon the altar of ambition, we have our firesides, our comfortable habitations, our cities, our churches and our country to defend, our rights, privileges and independence to preserve. And for these are we not justly contending? Thus it appears to me; yet I hear from our pulpits and read from our presses that it is an unjust, a wicked, a ruinous and unnecessary war. If I give an opinion with respect to the conduct of our native State, I cannot do it with approbation. She has had much to complain of as it respected a refusal of naval protection, yet that cannot justify her in paralyzing the arm of government when raised for her defence and that of the nation. A house divided against itself—and upon that foundation do our enemies build their hopes of subduing us. May it prove a sandy one to them.

"You once asked what does Mr. Adams think of Napoleon? The reply was, I think, that after having been the scourge of nations, he should himself be destroyed. We have seen him run an astonishing career. Is not his measure full? Like Charles the XII of Sweden, he may find in Alexander another Peter. Much, my friends, might we moralize upon these great events, but we know but in part and we see but in part. The longer I live, the more wrapt in clouds and darkness does the future appear to me."

British cruisers patrolled the New England coast, and could frequently be seen from the upper windows of the Quincy houses. If Mrs. Adams had climbed Penn's Hill on June 1st, 1813, she could have watched the naval duel between the *Chesapeake* and the *Shannon,* as in 1776 she had watched the burning of Charlestown.

A few months later, the neighborhood of Boston assumed once more the military aspect of forty years before. "Troops from Berkshire were quartered in Dorchester, at Neponset Bridge, generally considered the last outpost toward the enemy, who, it was thought, would land on Mr. Quincy's farm. One Sunday, a report came that the British had actually landed at Scituate, and were marching up to Boston. The drums beat to arms; and the elders, who remembered the Revolution, increased the trepidation of their juniors by anecdotes of devastation. These apprehensions were much exaggerated." [2]

In the midst of these alarms, John and Abigail Adams celebrated their golden wedding. "Yesterday," she writes to a granddaughter on the 26th of October, 1814, "yesterday completes half a century since I entered the married state, then just your age. I have great cause of thankfulness, that I have lived so long and enjoyed so large a portion of happiness as has been my lot. The greatest source of unhappiness I have known in that period has arisen from the long and cruel separations which I was called, in a time of war and with a young family around me, to submit to."

In the same house, their son, John Quincy Adams,

[2] "Memoir of S. E. M. Quincy."

and their grandson Charles Francis Adams, were in time to celebrate their golden weddings; a notable series of festivals.

A member of the Adams family tells me the Second President "has the reputation in the family of being very high tempered, and it is said that when he wrote letters which his wife thought unwise, she would hold them back and give them to him a week or so later, saying she thought perhaps he would prefer to change them! The singular thing was that he apparently never resented the tampering with his correspondence."

There can be no stronger proof than this of the oneness of this remarkable couple. President John may have been high tempered, but I fancy there are few men of today who would receive with meekness such action on the part of their wives.

The winter of 1814-15 opened gloomily enough. There seemed no immediate prospect of peace. Accordingly, when, on the 14th day of February, 1815, the bells began to ring, people mercly said, "Fire!" and looked out of window for the smoke. There was no smoke till the bonfires sprang up at night. More and more joyfully the bells pealed, till all knew that the war was over, that peace had been declared. Boston and Quincy and all the other neighboring towns went mad with joy. "The whole population were abroad, all classes congratulating each other on the happy tidings. Almost every house displayed a flag. Drums beat; cannon fired; the military were in motion. Sailors in large sleds, each drawn by fifteen horses,—the word 'Peace' in capitals on the hat of the foremost man,—greeted everyone with loud huzzas. The joy and exultation were in proportion to the previous fear and despondency. It was a day never to be forgotten." [8]

There were to be no more alarms for Abigail Adams; no more thunder of cannon or marching of troops: the rest of her life was peace. She had the joy of welcoming her eldest son, after his foreign service of eight long years, and of seeing him appointed Secretary of State. This, her grandson thinks, was the crowning mercy of her life. A few years more, and she might have seen him exalted to the loftier office which his father had held; but this was not to be. In October, 1818, she was stricken with typhus fever; and on the 28th day of that month, she died.

In closing the record of such a life as this, one longs for some perfect tribute which may fitly sum

[8] "Memoir of S. E. M. Quincy."

it up. I find this tribute, in the words of Josiah Quincy: "Clear and shedding blessings to the last, her sun sank below the horizon, beaming with the same mild strength and pure radiance which distinguished its meridian."

Another beautiful word was that of President Kirkland of Harvard University, spoken at Mrs. Adams' funeral:

"Ye seek to mourn, bereaved friends, as becomes Christians, in a manner worthy of the person you lament. You do, then, bless the Giver of life, that the course of your endeared and honored friend was so long and so bright; that she entered so fully into the spirit of these injunctions which we have explained, and was a minister of blessings to all within her influence. You are soothed to reflect that she was sensible of the many tokens of divine goodness which marked her lot; that she received the good of her existence with a cheerful and grateful heart; that, when called to weep, she bore adversity with an equal mind; that she used the world as not abusing it to excess, improving well her time, talents, and opportunities, and, though desired longer in this world, was fitted for a better happiness than this world can give."

John Adams survived his dearest friend by eight

years, preserving his faculties to the last, clear-minded and vehement as on the day when he signed the Declaration of Independence. At noon on the fiftieth anniversary of the "day of deliverance," amid the "pomp and parade," the "shows, games, sports, guns, bells, bonfires, and illuminations," which he had bespoken for it, his valiant spirit passed from earth. His last words were, "Thomas Jefferson still survives!" This was not the case. His ancient colleague, at one time his bitter opponent, but of late years once more his affectionate friend, had died an hour before.

Husband and wife lie side by side, under the portico of the First Church of Quincy, a building given by Mr. Adams to his beloved town. On the walls of that church are inscribed their epitaphs, which may most fitly close this simple record.

LIBERTATEM, AMICITIAM, FIDEM, RETINEBIS

D. O. M.

BENEATH THESE WALLS
ARE DEPOSITED THE MORTAL REMAINS OF

JOHN ADAMS.

SON OF JOHN AND SUZANNA (BOYLSTON) ADAMS,
SECOND PRESIDENT OF THE UNITED STATES;
BORN $\frac{19}{30}$ OCTOBER, 1735.

ON THE FOURTH OF JULY, 1776,
HE PLEDGED HIS LIFE, FORTUNE, AND SACRED HONOR
TO THE

INDEPENDENCE OF HIS COUNTRY.

ON THE THIRD OF SEPTEMBER, 1783,
HE AFFIXED HIS SEAL TO THE DEFINITIVE TREATY WITH
GREAT BRITAIN,
WHICH ACKNOWLEDGED THAT INDEPENDENCE,
AND CONSUMMATED THE REDEMPTION OF HIS PLEDGE.
ON THE FOURTH OF JULY, 1826,
HE WAS SUMMONED
TO THE INDEPENDENCE OF IMMORTALITY,
AND TO THE

JUDGMENT OF HIS GOD.

THIS HOUSE WILL BEAR WITNESS TO HIS PIETY;
THIS TOWN, HIS BIRTHPLACE, TO HIS MUNIFICENCE;
HISTORY TO HIS PATRIOTISM;
POSTERITY TO THE DEPTH AND COMPASS OF HIS MIND.

AT HIS SIDE
SLEEPS, TILL THE TRUMP SHALL SOUND,

ABIGAIL,

HIS BELOVED AND ONLY WIFE,
DAUGHTER OF WILLIAM AND ELIZABETH (QUINCY) SMITH;
IN EVERY RELATION OF LIFE A PATTERN
OF FILIAL, CONJUGAL, MATERNAL, AND SOCIAL VIRTUE.
BORN NOVEMBER $\frac{11}{22}$, 1744,
DECEASED 28 OCTOBER, 1818,
AGED 74.

MARRIED 25 OCTOBER, 1764.
DURING AN UNION OF MORE THAN HALF A CENTURY
THEY SURVIVED, IN HARMONY OF SENTIMENT, PRINCIPLE,
AND AFFECTION,
THE TEMPESTS OF CIVIL COMMOTION;
MEETING UNDAUNTED AND SURMOUNTING
THE TERRORS AND TRIALS OF THAT REVOLUTION,
WHICH SECURED THE FREEDOM OF THEIR COUNTRY;
IMPROVED THE CONDITION OF THEIR TIMES;
AND BRIGHTENED THE PROSPECTS OF FUTURITY
TO THE RACE OF MAN UPON EARTH.

PILGRIM.

FROM LIVES THUS SPENT THY EARTHLY DUTIES LEARN;
FROM FANCY'S DREAMS TO ACTIVE VIRTUE TURN:
LET FREEDOM, FRIENDSHIP, FAITH, THY SOUL ENGAGE,
AND SERVE, LIKE THEM, THY COUNTRY AND THY AGE.

(7)